The Compleat
Day Trader

The Compleat Day Trader

Trading Systems, Strategies, Timing Indicators, and Analytical Methods

Jake Bernstein

McGraw-Hill, Inc.

New York   San Francisco   Washington, D.C.   Auckland   Bogotá
Caracas   Lisbon   London   Madrid   Mexico City   Milan
Montreal   New Delhi   San Juan   Singapore
Sydney   Tokyo   Toronto

Library of Congress Cataloging-in-Publication Data

Bernstein, Jacob, (date)
    The compleat day trader : trading systems, strategies, timing
indicators, and analytical methods. / Jake Bernstein.
        p.   cm.
    Includes index.
    ISBN 0-07-009251-6
    1. Futures.   2. Futures market.   I. Title.   II. Title: Day
trader.
HG6024.A3B478   1995
332.64′5—dc20   94-41343
                                                            CIP

    8 9 10 FGRFGR 9 9 8

ISBN 0-07-009251-6

*The sponsoring editor for this book was David Conti, the editing supervisor was Caroline R.
Levine, and the production supervisor was Pamela A. Pelton. This book was set in Palatino
by Donald A. Feldman of McGraw-Hill's Professional Book Group composition unit.*

Printed and bound by Quebecor.

 This book is printed on recycled, acid-free paper containing 10% post-
consumer waste.

McGraw-Hill books are available at special quantity discounts to use as premiums
and sales promotions, or for use in corporate training programs. For more information, please write to the Director of Special Sales, McGraw-Hill, Inc., 11 West
19th Street, New York, NY 10011. Or contact your local bookstore.

Contents

Preface

For many years, futures traders have been fascinated with the idea of day trading. Increased market volatility has created large intraday price swings which, in turn, have provided numerous opportunities for the day trader.

In addition to the increase in opportunities, the wide availability of relatively low-priced computers and software has helped narrow the gap between the professional day trader and the novice.

The book you are about to read contains many different methods of day trading. Take the time to learn, study, and track the methods. Then, after you have learned the techniques you want to use, begin trading. But don't plunge in before you have spent some time learning the methods.

One last point before you begin your reading. Do not believe for even one second that day trading is easy. Day trading may, in fact, be more difficult than position trading. In the final analysis day trading is not the proverbial "piece of cake" that so many traders seek. If anyone tells you that you can day trade your way to riches with little effort they're wrong. Day trading takes work, work, and more work. If you do the work, you'll reap the rewards. It's that simple and it's that complicated.

I wish you success in your venture. If I can be of assistance, please call or write me.

Jake Bernstein

Acknowledgments

I wish to extend a special word of thanks to Commodity Quote Graphics of Glenwood Springs, Colorado, for permission to reprint charts from their outstanding quotation/graphics hardware and software program, SYSTEM ONE. I have been a CQG customer for many years and find their services outstanding as well as especially useful for the purpose of day trading.

I am also indebted to Mr. Bill Cruz of Omega Research in Miami, Florida, for his assistance and permission to use reports generated by his excellent analytical and testing software programs, TradeStation and SystemWriter. Both programs make the job of historical testing and system development enjoyable and efficient.

Naturally, I owe considerable thanks to the many traders I've known through the years who have contributed to my knowledge of the markets. You all know who you are. I've learned from each and every one of you. My list is far too lengthy to include here; however, I am thankful to all who have touched my life with their opinions, suggestions, systems, methods, and timing indicators.

My hard-working office staff must also be commended for their efforts in the production of this book. I am not easy to work with. I change my mind too easily and too quickly although all turns out well in the long run. Special thanks to Linda, Denise, and Rob. Patrick gets an extra note of thanks for editing and pasting up the manuscript. And, of course, thanks to Chris for his programming work.

Special thanks go to Marilyn my office manager and right-hand person whose efforts to keep me organized and clear-thinking help keep me on track.

My partner in Bernstein/Silber Futures, Mark Silber, is always a great sounding board for new ideas. Fortunately, he rejects many ideas and accepts only the most promising.

My family, Linda, Elliott, Gitelle, and Sara deserve great thanks for their forbearance and willingness to share their time with my charts, systems, computers, and manuscripts.

Finally, my acknowledgments would not be complete without a nod to my dear pet pug dogs, Buddy, Puggly, Hercules, Cassie, Roxy, and Inky for the play time I stole from them.

Introduction

The world of futures trading has become increasingly dominated by short-term speculation. In the good old days, markets moved slowly and steadily toward their goals, or they continued in sideways trends for extended periods. This is not the case today. In fact, since the early 1970s, virtually all futures markets have become increasingly volatile, and the time window of market moves has steadily narrowed.

This is not to say that the old adage "the big money is made in the big pull" is no longer true. It's just as true today as it has always been. There will always be large, long-term market moves. What *has changed*, however, is that short-term volatility has become so significant as to necessitate the use of extremely large stop losses, thereby forcing traders to risk substantially larger amounts of capital than ever before. The big pull still provides outstanding opportunities, but it also entails larger risks than ever before.

Increased volatility is both a sinner and a saint. Although it has made trading with limited risk less possible, it has also brought with it a plethora of short-term trading opportunities. Significant profit potential now exists in virtually all markets. Prior to the aforementioned increase in volatility, the potential for profit from short-term and day trading did not exist other than for the floor trader. Now such opportunities are available to all traders. But with opportunity also comes risk—they are both sides of the same coin. Without risk there cannot be reward—without volatility there cannot be intraday opportunity.

The Forces Behind Increased Volatility

In addition to increased volatility, several fundamental factors have become powerful driving forces in the futures markets, forces which were not significant to any meaningful degree prior to the 1970s. Specifically, I refer to relatively low commissions and significant advances in personal computer technology.

Furthermore, the advent of negotiated brokerage commissions and discount brokerage services has opened a vast new area of opportunity for all futures and futures options traders. It is now possible for traders who do not seek the advice, input, and "full service" of a broker to pay greatly reduced commissions, thereby allowing for more active trading as well as trading for smaller price moves. Commission cost is the single largest overhead factor in futures trading. Commission has always been, and will always be a severely limiting bottom-line factor for the futures trader. Unfortunately most traders fail to realize this vital fact. Combined with losses due to system limitations, trader error, and slippage, commission costs add up quickly. At the end of the year traders are often taken aback with what they have paid out in commissions and fees.

With greatly reduced commissions, however, the short-term and day trader can now trade more actively, more profitably, and more aggressively. Discount commission costs must, therefore, be considered as one of the most important factors contributing to the growth of short-term and day trading since the 1980s.

The Computer Revolution and Trading

In addition to the radical restructuring of commission costs to retail (i.e., nonprofessional) traders, there has also been a revolution in computer software and hardware technology. Since the mid-1980s, home computers have become increasingly powerful, efficient, and affordable. The cost of owning a state-of-the-art personal computer system has steadily declined while quality and processing speeds have steadily risen. For several thousand dollars, one can acquire a computer so sophisticated that by 1983 standards, its cost would easily have approached the $100,000 mark if not more.

Computers, however, are only as good as the software that makes them productive. They are limited by the limitations of software programs. Computer software specifically designed for personal computers (PCs and Macintoshes) has also made tremendous gains, particularly since the late 1980s. Virtually no area of science, literature, mathematics, or investments has been left untouched by the quantum advances in sophisticated software. The combination of advanced computer hardware, high-level computer software, and low-cost computer memory have ushered in a new era of futures trading, which, to borrow a concept from J. Peter Steidlmayer, I call "the Age of Instantism."

Advances in Market Quotation Systems

Those who seek to venture into the new realm of instantism have at their disposal a multiplicity of market quotation services which provide everything from tick-by-tick data to delayed and after-market-closing data. Accurate price quotations at affordable prices are now available throughout the day for access by computer. The availability of live tick-by-tick data throughout the trading day has enhanced public participation in an area which for many years was the exclusive domain of professional off-the-floor traders as well as on-the-floor pit brokers. And this has added to the pool of short-term and day-trading participants. This, in turn, has increased liquidity which has facilitated short-term and day trading.

The International and Domestic Political Backdrop

While the aforementioned technical and fundamental factors have helped accelerate the tremendous growth of short-term and day trading in the futures market since the early 1980s, the backdrop of worldwide and domestic political and economic instability has exerted a synergistic force in markets already stimulated to greater activity. The uncertainty which originated during the OPEC oil embargo has spread its effect to virtually all markets during the last 20 years. Barely a market has been left untouched by international political instability and machinations.

Since the economic peak in the United States occurred between 1975 and 1981, the stability of once-revered domestic economic institutions has been seriously threatened, forcing an understandable deterioration of trader and investor confidence. Insecurities have expressed themselves in highly emotional markets and in extremely violent price moves within relatively circumscribed periods.

The exaggerated price movements which occurred during the stock market crashes of 1987 and 1989, as well as the minicrash of 1992 were symptomatic of underlying trader anxiety motivated by panic. The panics were clearly the result of diminished confidence in existing institutions and in the ability of government to regulate economic affairs.

Responsibilities and Goals of the Day Trader

My task is not to analyze or moralize about the multiplicity of factors which have stimulated the growth of short-term and day trading, rather it is to accept the facts as they are and to teach you how you may take advantage of them for the purposes of day trading. It is not the job of the day trader to understand the whys and/or the wherefores of market movement. The day trader's sole responsibilities are these:

✓ *First* to end each day "flat," that is, without any positions
✓ *Second*, to make a profit, no matter how large or small
✓ *Third*, to keep all losses small and manageable

Within the context of these very general responsibilities and guidelines for the day trader, all market volatility, regardless of cause, must be approached as an opportunity for potential profit. We are neither defenders of what is right or just in the markets nor pedagogues who must determine why things are the way they are. We are interested in being true to our tripartite credo as expressed above and in attaining three distinct goals which are the essence of what this book is designed to teach you. These goals are as follows:

1. To profit consistently and significantly from day trading
2. To become better day traders with more experience
3. To maintain a disciplined and business-oriented approach to help attain day-trading objectives

About This Book

The purpose of this book is to acquaint all day traders, aspiring day traders, and other interested parties with the basics of successful day trading. My goal is to expand considerably on the basic day-trading building blocks, in order to provide concise methods, indicators, and guidelines, which, it is hoped, will prove beneficial on the road to profits. Please note that this book *is not designed to serve as a cookbook or "no brain" approach to day trading.* I am absolutely convinced, after my many years of experience as a trader, that *effective trading can be learned and moreover that many traders are quite capable of learning to be effective.* One of the prerequisites, however, is to learn from a teacher who is organized, experienced, lucid, and, above all, specific.

My experiences as a trader have led me to the conclusion that *successful day trading is built upon a unique foundation combining art and science.* If pressed to "guesstimate" as to the proper mix of both qualities, I'd say that approximately 70 percent of successful day trading consists of technique or science and 30 percent of skill and/or art. This, however, would be a misleading statement inasmuch as both elements are symbiotic;

without one, the other would be ineffective. The successful day trader combines both elements synergistically to produce profits, consistency, and longevity.

Beware of Tall Tales

Even if you're a newcomer to the futures markets, you have likely been exposed to the numerous tall tales of great successes by novice traders or by those who have discovered hot new systems. This is all old stuff. Such tales have existed since the first trader traded the first futures contract. And they will exist as long as there are markets to trade and traders to trade them. Don't bother chasing these dead ends—they will lead you astray. Also, don't compete with any of them, they will lead you, more often than not, to frustration and losses.

My best advice is to compete only with yourself. If you attempt to play others' games by their rules, you will frequently be a loser. The quintessential element of successful day trading is to *find something that you can do well and do it consistently day in and day out.* I don't mean to imply by any means that day trading is an effortless proposition or that it is something as simple as finding a good bread recipe and following it.

Who Succeeds and Who Fails—Qualities for Success

Clearly, day trading is not for everyone. Certain qualities predispose a day trader to success or failure. Before we go on with a concise discussion of the techniques, systems, and methods of day trading which I've acquired by long and hard experience through the years, I'd like to familiarize you with the qualities which either facilitate or limit one's success as a day trader. Many of the things I am about to say apply to success not only in the markets but in every walk of life as well.

To be successful in virtually any human endeavor requires a number of skills which are not easily acquired. Although the struggle to achieve these skills may indeed be an arduous one, the effort is worthwhile both in the long run and in the short run. I say this because there is a great deal of transference in skills across many different professions and undertakings. This does not necessarily mean, however, that a good engineer will become a good trader. Nor does it mean that a bad engineer will become a bad trader. It's been my observation that choice of profession is not closely correlated with probability of success in the futures markets. Here is a list of qualities I feel are essential to success as a trader.

Flexibility

I have observed that extremely rigid personality types tend to perform poorly as futures traders inasmuch as they have not mastered the ability to think beyond the rules, a skill which is extremely important for the day trader. You will find most often that market entry is very specific and not subject to a great deal of interpretation, if any. Market exit however, is frequently more intuitive, although it can be subjected to more definitive and operational procedures. Consequently, when I refer to such qualities as discipline, persistence, organization, and the ability to follow through, I am not referring to any of these in rigid terms.

Perhaps the greatest single quality a day trader should possess is flexibility or adaptability. Such flexibility, however, must be maintained within the context of specific understandings, trading signals, and/or guidelines which are the subject matter of this book. *A trader must be flexible not only to new ideas about the markets, but also to situations which develop in markets during the day.* Hence, flexibility is an important quality which, unfortunately, cannot be taught. I can, however, give you some specific ideas about flexibility so that you may make the necessary adjustments to your own trading style.

Perhaps a better way to express this is by saying that *in order to be a successful day trader, you must be "flexible but firm."* In other words, you must understand the rules, the signals, and the timing indicators. However, you must apply them in a manner which is mediated by other understandings about yourself and about the markets. I will attempt to clarify this for you in the chapters which follow.

Consistency

Another important quality which the successful day trader must either possess or develop is consistency. By consistency, I mean *the ability and willingness to follow a particular program or trading methodology day in and day out as long as the technique continues to achieve the desired results.* In other words, if something you learn in this book or elsewhere is working for you, then continue to use it until it no longer works or until you suspect that it is slowly but surely becoming ineffective. *Too many day traders spend too much of their time attempting to improve on methods which cannot be improved.* The fact is, not too many methods work consistently well in the markets, and, furthermore, those which do work well cannot be improved beyond a certain point. *"If it ain't broke...don't fix it."* Consistency is a very important quality which must be cultivated if day trading is to become a successful proposition.

Patience

Patience is yet another important virtue. *Day traders must be willing and able to tolerate a series of losses, as they patiently await a turn in their fortune. However, too much patience is not a virtue for the day trader. Too much patience can be a fatal flaw.* The day trader who is too patient in hanging on to a losing position will be violating one of the cardinal rules of successful day trading, which is, of course, not to carry losing positions (or for that matter any positions) overnight. Losses must, in all cases, be taken as quickly and as expeditiously as possible. The idea is, of course, to ride profits to their maximum while eliminating losses quickly and at the smallest dollar amount.

Self-Control

Another important quality which successful day traders must either possess or develop is self-control. During any given day, literally hundreds of day-trading opportunities will present themselves. Whereas many of these may turn out to be profitable opportunities, the day trader does not know in advance which will or will not produce the desired results. The vast majority of opportunities are specious.

Furthermore, the day trader is limited in how many of these opportunities may be taken. It behooves the day trader, therefore, to begin each day's trading with a general plan of action within which the day's events may be interpreted and the proper actions taken. The plan, however, must not be so restrictive as to blind the trader to other unexpected opportunities. In so doing, some of the worthless or losing opportunities will be eliminated ahead of time, and the trader will stay focused on those which seem to offer the best potential.

Hopefully, the information contained in this book will be valuable to you in making these decisions. I liken the job of the day trader to that of a hunter. The day trader and the hunter are both provided with a finite amount of ammunition. For the hunter, the ammunition consists of bullets, arrows, or weapons. The day trader's ammunition is capital. Trading capital and ammunition may both be easily squandered in pursuit of worthless targets, and the trader and hunter who engage in this type of useless activity will eventually find themselves without the ammunition to pursue larger, more profitable game. The day trader must be patient, methodically awaiting only the more promising opportunities upon which to take aim and fire. And then, when the opportunity presents itself, the trader must follow through according to plan.

Willingness to Exit Trades at End of Day

Still another important quality which the day trader must develop is the willingness to exit positions by the end of the day. Veteran futures traders jokingly define long-term positions as "day trades which ended the day at a loss." The lesson here is that all too many traders enter positions originally as day trades; however, if these trades show losses at the end of the day, they are inclined to hold them overnight or longer given their refusal to take the loss. The justification or excuse is that the trade probably has more than mere day-trade value. *Holding a position overnight, particularly a losing position, is perhaps the single greatest offense that a day trader can commit.* Frequently, it is also the single most costly violation of the rules.

Accepting Losses

The successful day trader must learn how to accept a loss and when to recognize that this rule is being violated. There are some very specific and simple procedures for doing this which will be discussed later on. The day trader must be willing to accept what he or she has achieved by the end of each day without undue frustration and/or wishful thinking—win, lose, or draw. As human beings we always look back on what we have done, often with regrets, thinking that we should have done things differently. Although in many cases it is certainly true that things should have been done differently, lamenting that fact is not constructive. Learning from it, however, is the appropriate response. *Each loss, if taken at the right time, is a lesson.* Each loss will teach you something important. If the amount of the loss is approximately what it should have been in terms of your system or method, then you have learned that you can follow your system. If, however, your loss is not taken on time and therefore becomes larger than it might have been, then you have learned that *to go against your system will cost you money.*

Daily Analysis of Results

Day traders should have a formal procedure for analyzing their results at the end of each day in order that the maximum amount of learning be extracted from each trade, whether that trade was a profit or a loss. This, of course, requires some degree of organization and consistency. I will discuss the importance of your trading diary in considerable detail later on. At this time I urge you to begin keeping a diary if you are not already doing so. You'll be absolutely amazed how much you can learn by jotting down your comments at the end of each trading day (or preferably during the day). It only takes a few minutes, and the reward is literally hundreds of times the cost.

What This Book Cannot and Will Not Do for You

Some authors are quite accomplished at telling you what their book will do for you. I would prefer to tell you not only what this book can do for you, but moreover *what it cannot and will not do for you.* I do this at the outset so that you will not revel in any unrealistic expectations or unwarranted fantasies about what you will read within these pages. This book, in and of itself, *is not a treasure map to riches untold or a handy little instruction book to the secrets of trading success.* While it *does* contain many of my secrets as well as extremely valuable information, secrets without action, or valuable information without direction and consistency are nothing more than lifeless exhibits at a museum.

Within these pages you will find *no claims that this book alone will be a vehicle for your attainment of great wealth as a day trader.* If you are looking for guarantees, you'll need to look elsewhere because you won't find them in this book. I will only guarantee you that the ideas, systems, methods, indicators, and suggestions in this book will give you the potential to achieve success, *but you, and you alone are the instrument which will transform potential energy into actual energy.*

If you seek to acquire the substantial knowledge which I have accrued during my more than 22 years as a futures and stock trader, then you've certainly come to the right place. This book will educate you, guide you, assist you, explain things to you, and illuminate the way for you. But it will not trade for you, put money in your pocket or in your bank account, nor will it fill your head with misleading guarantees. I can teach you how to ride the bicycle, but I cannot ride it for you.

Any individual who has had experience as a trader, albeit limited, learns very early in the game that to achieve consistent success in futures trading is possibly one of the most difficult undertakings a human being can attempt. Success comes only to a few. The reasons for this will be explained clearly and carefully in the chapters which follow. I will demonstrate that the difficulty in attaining success as a trader is primarily one of the trader as opposed to the system or method. It is my goal to facilitate success for you *by teaching you techniques as well as methods for improving the self, in the hope that you will eventually join the ranks of those who are successful day traders.*

No Exaggerated Claims

Furthermore, I do not make any exaggerated claims about what you can achieve as a day trader. Although "the sky's the limit" in futures trading, it is up to the individual trader to maximize what can be achieved. I am only a guide who can teach you techniques which I've found useful during my years as a trader. There are no unrealistic claims in this book. If you want those, you'll have to read some of the magazines which help perpetuate such rubbish...or you'll have to read some of your junk mail. If anything, I've attempted to tone down all claims so that when you achieve success you'll be very pleasantly surprised. I'd rather have you keep your expectations low so that you will be happy with what you achieve. For too many years too many unscrupulous operators have preyed upon the public, asserting absurdly fantastic claims, pandering to the weaknesses of human greed and hope. You'll find none of that in this book.

Historical Results

Throughout the book you will find references to historical results or to statistical summaries. Unless otherwise stated, these are as up-to-date as possible to the time of this writing. I warn you that with time, these statistics will change. They should therefore be updated either through your own research or by consulting with my office. Should you have a question regarding their current applicability, please don't hesitate to contact me.

Note also that my examples are taken primarily from current market activity. I could easily hunt and search for historical examples which illustrate my points perfectly. These would, however, be textbook cases and, therefore, misleading. The reality of day trading, indeed, of all trading is that nothing works as well in reality as it does on paper. This is a fact which I must emphasize early and often so that you will, above all, emerge from this book as a realist.

Do Your Own Research

I always encourage individual research by traders. There are so many ideas which can be applied to today's futures markets that any one individual does not have a monopoly on research. In fact, every trader is so very different in his or her perceptions of the markets that distinctly different methodologies and applications will be visualized and developed by different traders. Some of the ideas presented in this book may spark in your mind concepts and methods which could prove highly profitable. Don't allow yourself to be restricted or encumbered by my words, rather use my work as a starting point for your own good research. Certainly if you find that my techniques are working for you, then continue to use them and adapt them to serve your own purposes.

I always look forward to hearing from my readers, particularly if they have feedback on the techniques I've taught and/or if they have developed new methodologies which improve upon those suggested in my books. If you have developed your own trading methods and are willing to share them, then I most certainly invite you to get in touch with me.

Practice

Practice is extremely important. It is absolutely necessary if you are to fully implement the indicators, concepts, and topics discussed in this book. I urge you to practice in real time as soon and as often as you can. Learning to day trade from a book is very much like learning to ride a bicycle from a book. None of what I am about to teach you will crystallize into profitable action until you get on the bicycle and begin to ride it. Hopefully you will not have to fall off the bicycle too many times before you understand the actions which go along with my words.

Getting Started

Aside from the motivation and persistence which are required for success in any venture, you will not need any other tools in order to get started with this book. I will make a few suggestions however which may prove valuable.

1. *Read slowly.* Although you may feel that the subject matter is very straightforward and simple, please read through it slowly, first for the general idea, and then a second or third time for the specifics.
2. *Apply your knowledge to the examples.* Where I have provided examples, I urge you to apply what you have learned in order to make certain you understand it.
3. *Take notes.* I also urge you to take notes both in the margins of this text and on a separate notepad. The material will be easier for you to comprehend and retain if you take notes.
4. *Take your learning to the markets.* Once you have internalized the concepts, please observe them under real market conditions to determine

how well they work for you and if they are consistent with your needs as a trader.

Risk and Loss in Futures Trading

The regulatory agencies which oversee the futures markets, namely the Commodity Futures Trading Commission and the National Futures Association, have imposed certain specific requirements on those who are members of these organizations. Failure to comply with the regulations of these agencies can result in expulsion from membership, reprimand, and/or monetary penalties. Although I am certain you are all already aware of this fact, I am required, therefore, to warn you and remind you (in case you didn't already know) that *there is a risk of loss in futures trading.*

I am also required by law to give you the following disclaimer.

> The CFTC requires we state that—notice: Hypothetical or simulated performance results have certain limitations. Unlike an actual performance record, simulated results do not represent actual trading. Also since the trades have not actually been executed, the results may have under- or over-compensated for the impact, if any, of certain market factors, such as lack of liquidity. Simulated trading programs in general are also subject to the fact that they are designed with the benefit of hindsight. No representation is being made that any account will or is likely to achieve profits or losses similar to those shown. The risk of loss in futures trading can be substantial. You should carefully consider whether such trading is suitable for you in light of your financial condition. Past results are not indicative of future results. There is a risk of loss in futures trading

Furthermore, I am also required to mention repeatedly the potential for risk whenever the potential for profit is mentioned throughout the course of this book. I feel that all of you already know the risks, and I resent having to repeat them. It is a waste of space and time, and it is an insult to your intelligence and mine. Consequently, I will do so, not by choice, but by the necessity of regulatory dictate.

1
The Basics

Before digging too deeply into the technical aspects of day trading, we'll need to examine some housekeeping details which pertain to our task. First among these is a brief but necessary definition of terms. The futures markets have their own language without which they could not function and without which you will be unable to trade. So let's take a look at some important terminology which will be used throughout the text. These terms are not presented in any order other than, perhaps, frequency of use.

Definition of Terms

Day Trading, Day Trader. In order to avoid confusion or misunderstandings, I'll first define for you the terms *day trading* and *day trader*. Although you may think that this is an unnecessary waste of time and space, I cannot tell you how surprised I am at the all-too-common lack of knowledge which most individuals have about day trading, what it is and what it is designed to achieve.

A day trade is a *trade which is entered and exited on the same day*. It does not mean that the trade will be held overnight, that it will be kept overnight if profitable, that it will always be entered on the opening and exited on the close, or that it will not entail risk. Day trades are always over by the end of the trading day. By definition they are no longer day trades if carried through to the next trading session. True day traders will not hold positions to the next trading session regardless of how they have fared during the day. Succinctly this means that a loss is a loss and a profit is a profit and that all scores are settled by the end of the trading session—win, lose, or draw. Day trades may be entered at any time during the day, but they must be closed out by the end of the day.

Position Trader, Position Trading.   A day trader is one who day trades. As soon as a day trader holds a position overnight, he or she cannot refer to the trade as a day trade or to him or herself as a day trader. A position trader, however, holds trades for an extended period. The position trader in futures is like the investor in stocks, albeit with a shorter time perspective, which is not necessarily limited by the life of the futures contract.

There is no crime in being a position trader and certainly no crime or embarrassment in being a day trader. However, you must be careful what you tell yourself, or you may begin to believe it. A day trader is an individual who is committed to a certain specific course of action. To sway from this course of action is to subvert the program. To stray from the program is to abandon its principles and to acquire a new set of expectations which may not be consistent with the original objective. I urge you, therefore, to be committed to your course of action once you have determined it.

If you wish to be a position trader, then do yourself a service and do not refer to yourself as a day trader, lest you confuse your objectives. Simply stated, what's right for the position trader is not necessarily right for the day trader and vice versa. Position traders may be willing, for example, to carry a losing position for quite some time in the expectation that it will eventually become profitable. To the day trader, this is a violation of the cardinal rule.

Is it not possible, you ask, for traders to wear different hats at different times or many hats at the same time? Absolutely! There is nothing wrong with trading in many different time frames at the same time, provided you do so with specific structure and follow specific rules which will be explained to you later on in this book. But remember, this book is primarily, in fact, exclusively, for the day trader.

Short-Term Trading, Short-Term Trader.   A short-term trader as opposed to a day trader or a position trader is one who trades for relatively short-term market swings of 2 to 10 days' duration. There is no firm definition of the exact length of time short-term traders hold their positions. The distinction between a short-term trader and a position trader is not as precise as is the distinction between a day trader and all other types of traders. A day trader trades within the day time frame as a hard and fast rule, whereas position traders' and short-term traders' time lengths are not as specifically defined. Many of the techniques described in this book may be applied to short-term trading as well as day trading. For those interested in learning short-term trading systems and methods, I recommend my book *Short Term Trading in Futures* (Probus Books, Chicago). It is available through my office.

Intermediate-Term Trading. An intermediate-term trade is one usually held for several months. Such trades are preferred by many traders, money managers, and investors. Intermediate-term traders seek to take advantage of larger price swings.

Long-Term Trading. In reality there are very few long-term futures traders. A long-term trader may hold positions for several years, rolling contracts forward as they approach expiration. What the day trader does is the complete antithesis of what the long-term trader does. For those interested in long-term trading I recommend my book, *Long Term Trading in Futures*, available from my office.

Slippage. Slippage is the tendency of a market to fall or rise very quickly, picking buy and sell stop orders very quickly. Hence, when I refer to a $100 deduction for slippage, I mean that I am deducting $100 from every trade in a hypothetical back test in order to represent more accurately what might have happened. A market which tends to have too much slippage is, therefore, a market in which quick and sudden price moves tend to result in price fills which are unexpectedly or unreasonably far away from your price orders.

Trading Systems. A trading system, as opposed to a trading method, timing indicator, trading technique, market pattern, and so on, is an organized methodology containing specific market entry and exit indicators, as well as an operational set of procedures (called *rules*) including, but not limited to, various risk management (follow-up stop-loss procedures) methods and procedures. A trading system is implemented by following specific timing signals which dictate market entry and exit. I am defining this term specifically here in order to distinguish a trading system from other market techniques which are not as specific and/or which do not follow a predetermined set of procedures.

Trading systems must be necessarily rigid in their construction for the purpose of delineating specific procedures which, theoretically, should lead to profitable trading, provided the system is functioning as intended or tested. *In practice, most traders do not follow a trading system. They delude themselves into thinking that they are trading according to a system, however, they violate the rules of their own trading systems so frequently that one ought not term their actions systematic.* This definition is designed to set the stage for more extensive commentary on the subject in a later chapter.

In closing this brief definition I reiterate that *a trading system must be systematic or it is not a trading system, regardless of what the individual who professes to be trading a "system" may think.* A few traders actually follow trading systems. The vast majority of traders begin with a system but alter it to suit their internal feelings about the markets to the extent that they are not following a system at all other than, perhaps, in their own minds.

Timing Indicators, Timing Signals.   A timing indicator is defined as any specific technique, whether fundamental or technical which objectively indicates market entry, exit, or the underlying condition (i.e., bullish, bearish, neutral) of a given market or markets. A timing indicator can also be called a *timing signal.* I will use the terms interchangeably.

The definition given above is intentionally general for the specific purposes of this book. You will find, in later chapters, that literally thousands of timing indicators may be used in many different ways. Timing indicators must be objective, that is, *not subject to interpretation.* An indicator which is subject to interpretation is not an indicator, it is, rather, a technique and, therefore, subject to different interpretations by different traders and even by the same trader in different situations. I will make every effort in this book to differentiate among timing indicators, trading techniques, and trading methods.

Trading Technique.   A trading technique as opposed to a timing indicator, timing signal, or trading system is a fairly loose collection of procedures which assists traders in making decisions about market entry or exit. Frequently a trading technique consists of one or more timing indicators combined with general entry and exit rules and/or risk management procedures. A trading technique is, therefore, not a trading system but rather an approach to trading which is generally objective but not nearly as precise or rigid as is a trading system.

In practice, most traders follow techniques as opposed to systems. Much of what you will learn in this book relates specifically to trading techniques; however, I have also included some of my favorite trading systems. A trading system can be used as a trading technique if you wish. As I pointed out earlier, this is in fact what most day traders and most position traders actually do.

Market Entry and Exit.   All traders should be familiar with these terms. Do not bother reading this definition if you are already familiar with these terms. *Market entry* means simply to establish a new long, short, or spread position. *Market exit* means to close out an existing long, short, or spread position. There are many different types of orders which may be used for entering and exiting markets. These are discussed later on.

Optimization, Curve Fitting. The act of fitting a trading system to past data is called *optimizing*. When a trading system developer optimizes a system, he or she does so in order to generate a set of system rules which have performed well on historical data. Although the system appears to have worked well in the past, it is in fact "fitted" to the data. Hence, the system will frequently not perform well in the future. To a given extent, most system testing involves some degree of optimization or curve fitting. Although opinions on curve fitting differ sharply among market experts, I caution you to avoid such systems.

These, then, are some of the very general terms which I will use throughout the course of this book. Terms not noted herein will be defined as they are introduced. Please note that my intent in redefining terms which you may already know is *not to insult your intelligence* but rather to make absolutely certain that we are communicating, since this is of paramount importance when teaching specific trading systems techniques and methods. Furthermore, many terms commonly used nowadays are not clearly understood by the individuals using them.

2
What a Day Trader Is; What a Day Trader Does

Perhaps the single most important issue at the outset is to define exactly what I mean when I use the terms *day trader* and *day trading.* It will be in our best interest to define what the day trader does to make certain that you learn the skills you need to succeed in this highly demanding task.

A day trader trades strictly within the day time frame. The day trader, therefore, establishes positions at some time within the day and *always* exits these positions by the end of the trading session. Failure to exit positions by the end of the trading session violates the single most important rule of day trading. The day trader who does not exit positions by the end of the trading session is not therefore a day trader. I emphasize this point inasmuch as there are many individuals who wish to day trade but who, for lack of discipline, cannot do so effectively or consistently.

To carry a trade beyond the close of trading on the day of entry is to *violate not only the cardinal rule of day trading but also to destroy the advantage that day trading offers over all other forms of trading.* You may find my insistence that a day trader only trade within the time frame of the day somewhat annoying, but I must emphasize this point strongly. I will do so repeatedly in order to impress upon you the importance of staying with your primary goal as a day trader.

For those who insist on violating the rules, I will provide some sensible alternatives and procedures which should prove helpful. I do, however, insist that positions entered as day trades be closed out as day trades with very few exceptions to this rule. Since a day trader is one who trades within the day time frame, day trading is the job of the day trader.

What Does a Day Trader Trade?

Although some would argue that only certain markets are amenable to day trading, I disagree. *At some time or another all markets are suitable for day trading, provided that certain conditions are met.* I will teach how to recognize which markets to day trade and when to day trade them. Regardless of which markets are traded, the day trader will adhere strictly to the policy of entering and exiting positions within the day time frame.

Some markets lend themselves more readily to certain trading systems, methods, and techniques. I will identify these for you. Some day traders will avoid certain markets, feeling, perhaps, that the potential for profit is not large enough or that risk is too high. This is not necessarily true. The only thing which should dissuade a day trader from trading certain markets is lack of liquidity. I will be more specific later. For now, however, suffice it to say that all reasonably active futures markets have potential to be day traded at one time or another. There are some markets which are suitable for day trading almost every day, and some markets should be day traded only at certain times. I will tell you how to know when given markets should be day traded and when they should not.

Why Day Trade?

Given the volatile market environment which I have previously described, day trading offers many advantages over position trading, although day trading is not recommended for all traders. Several particularly cogent reasons support day trading as a viable orientation within the limitations which will be presented later.

1. Maximized Equity

Day trading allows traders to maximize their trading capital by avoiding the need to post overnight margins. Many brokerage firms will allow traders to trade actively and very aggressively within the day time frame, provided these individuals have the financial resources, the demonstrated responsibility, and the maturity to do so. If your broker and/or brokerage firm has the confidence that you will not accumulate a large deficit, you will be permitted to trade many markets, and fairly large positions during the day, without needing to post the large margin requirements which would be necessary if the positions were held overnight.

It is therefore possible for a trader to maintain a relatively small cash balance in his or her account and to day trade considerably larger quantities in terms of total number of contracts than might be the case were it not for day trading.

2. Reduced Risk Exposure

Although some individuals would vehemently argue this point, I maintain that day trading affords less exposure to the risk of loss than does position trading. The position trader is often a victim of considerable price volatility which results from news or fundamental developments occurring after trading hours. It is not uncommon for a position trader to find that a trade which showed considerable profit at the end of the previous trading session shows a substantial loss on the opening of the next trading session as a result of overnight news or market-related developments.

This is, of course, a two-sided coin (it can work for you or against you), but it is far better to avoid the exposure of risk than to gamble on overnight news. Certainly news can occur during the trading day; however, the day trader can respond within the day time frame, since the markets are open and the position can be closed out. In other words, news can be used to the advantage of the trader or to indicate that the day trade should be closed out.

Opening price gaps, although potentially negative for position traders can be used to the advantage of the day trader. Although these gaps frequently work to the disadvantage of the position trader, there are opening price gap methods (to be discussed later) which provide many profitable opportunities to the day trader, opportunities which are either unavailable to the position trader or which are actually injurious to the position trader.

3. Advantages of Forced Exit

Day trading forces traders who follow their rules to exit positions by the end of the day, win, lose, or draw. This, in effect, forces traders to take their losses no matter what excuses may be conjured up in favor of holding positions. Consequently, a day trader who holds a position beyond the close of trading knows that he or she has broken one of the cardinal rules of day trading and that the consequences may be negative.

I do not suggest, by any means, that positions which show a loss at the end of the day and which are then held through to the next trading session invariably show a loss the next day. The odds are probably 50/50.

However, losses are frequently larger than profits, and, furthermore, carrying a position overnight leaves the day trader uncertain as to what should be done the next day. This is why the day trader who follows the rules will be spared the pain of loss as well as the often debilitating anxiety and uncertainty which are part and parcel of riding losses.

Those who are committed to day trading and who follow the rules accordingly will not carry losing positions overnight and, in so doing, will avoid one of the most serious problems traders encounter in their speculative ventures. It is far better to close out a position, even at a loss, if this will prevent the loss from becoming larger the next day.

4. Reliability of Timing Signals

A third reason for considering day trading is that many signals and trading systems appear to be more reliable in shorter time frames than they do in longer-term time frames. I find it considerably less difficult to develop trading systems, methods, and timing indicators which are more accurate within the day time frame than indicators which attempt to trade for intermediate-term moves. As a point of information, I have also found more trading systems and timing methods that work well on a *very long term basis* than those which work well in the intermediate term.

5. Immediate Feedback

Another substantial benefit of day trading is the fact that feedback in the form of profits or losses is much quicker than it is in the case of position trades. This is important to the trader who is concerned about learning from his or her errors (i.e., losses). A position trader who enters a bad trade may not get feedback (in the form of a loss) until many weeks, possibly months, later. The day trader, however, will know no later than the end of the day and frequently within minutes or even seconds that the trade is not a profitable one. Such positive or negative reinforcement (in the Skinnerian sense) is important in learning how to trade. Frequently, position traders will close out a losing trade so long after the position was entered that the original reason for entry has been forgotten (or repressed), and, therefore, very little if anything can be learned from the loss.

6. Faster Development Time

A day-trading system can be tested and developed in real time more quickly than can a position-trading system. The availability of continuous contract, tick-by-tick data makes system testing by computer faster and, I feel, easier. It is possible to test literally thousands of cases. This increases the statistical reliability of test results.

7. Trader Personality

A less technical reason for preferring day trading relates to the personality of the trader. I find day trading to be considerably more enjoyable and frankly much less stressful than carrying positions overnight. Some methods of day trading are more time- and attention-intensive than position trading, but there is a certain pleasure derived from knowing that no positions are kept overnight and that any unexpected international or domestic developments cannot impact me, since I do not have any open positions. Day trading appeals to certain individuals such as yourself. It is probably more closely suited to your specific needs than are either position trading or short-term trading. That's why you're reading this book.

In Summary

In summary, the day trader seeks to capitalize on moves which occur within the day time frame. Many techniques may be used, but many, unfortunately, prove to be nothing but blind alleys. The rest of this book goes on to teach and explain some of the methods I've developed over the years. Some of my techniques are highly specific and objective; others are more subjective and fall into the category of trading methods or techniques as opposed to systems. The day-trading methods and systems which follow are ones which I've developed during my more than 20 years as a futures trader. I sincerely believe that those who take the time to learn them, to use them, and to refine them will benefit handsomely.

3

The Illusion of
System Testing

There is perhaps, no other area in the field of futures trading which has been as abused or as misrepresented as trading system development. Futures traders generally pride themselves on being a group of objective, analytical, and logical people. They gloat in their skepticism and dogged insistence upon scientific validation of trading methodologies. Wherever possible, they insist upon the hard facts of system performance. This orientation to the validation of futures trading systems and methods has been growing in intensity and popularity since the advent of affordable computer hardware and software.

A number of authors, of whom the most prominent is Perry Kaufmann, have written extensively on the subject of system testing and system development. Great emphasis has been placed upon the importance of adequately testing trading systems in order to validate their use in real time. Furthermore, the area of system optimization has received considerable attention as well. Both areas should be studied carefully by serious futures traders, since the issues involved are likely to significantly impact the systems and methods you trade as well as your market performance. Perhaps my input will assist you. Possibly you may not agree with everything I'm saying. But my words come from the voice of experience—experience which spans nearly one-quarter of a century in the futures markets. First, let's deal with the issue of system development.

System Development

With a few thousand dollars' worth of computer software and hardware, it is now possible for virtually any semi-computer-literate individual to develop seemingly profitable trading systems. I use the words "seemingly profitable" because, in my experience, the development of trading systems which have shown profitable back-tested results *does not in any way, shape, or form guarantee that these results will be reproducible in the future under real-time market conditions*. Please note a system test is merely *the analysis of a particular model which is imposed upon the market*. The more complex the model, the more it will reflect a fit of the past data, but this fit is not necessarily applicable to future market conditions.

Curve fitting, as the procedure of developing seemingly effective trading systems is called, can produce spectacular results which are nothing but hypothetical and which have no bearing whatsoever on the future. Hence, system testing deserves attention and close scrutiny if test results are to be taken seriously and used for the purpose of actual trading.

Several important issues must be understood if you are to avoid the trap of trading based on system tests. I realize that my point of view regarding the issues of systems, system testing, and system optimization will not be shared by all readers or for that matter by all traders or market analysts. I feel it is necessary, nevertheless, for me to express these ideas so that you will, hopefully, achieve a better understanding of my orientation to the markets, and to trading futures. You will find that my point of view regarding the subject of system development is not nearly as rigid or institutionalized as is the current thinking of my colleagues. *Although I am not opposed to system testing, I do believe that there are inherent dangers in taking the results of system tests too literally.* Let me explain what I mean.

What Is a Trading System?

A trading system is merely an approach to organizing facts and understanding relationships about markets. Presumably, the idea behind a trading system is to arrive at a series of steps which, generally translated, result in expectations based on if-then scenarios. It is presumed that by following the procedures and rules of a trading system which has been effectively back-tested, the trader will, assuming perfect adherence to the rules, produce profitable results. At the very least, it is hoped that the trader will stand a better chance of profiting through the use of a trading system than through the use of no system.

I have serious doubts about both assumptions. Here's why. A trading system is developed by imposing a hypothetical and artificial framework upon a set of data which has a considerable amount of built-in random behavior. The course of trading system development consists of trial and error until an effective combination of market indicators has been ascertained. These indicators, frequently combined with principles of risk management, purportedly indicate what would have happened historically had they been applied to the particular market or markets. In the vast majority of cases, the trading system themselves *do not reveal any underlying truths or realities about the markets but rather reveal that a superficially imposed set of rules can result in acceptable results provided the two essential elements of all trading are contained within that system.* And these two elements are *the limitation of losses and the maximization of profits.*

In other words, extensive system testing reveals that the vast majority of trading systems produce results which are accurate 50 percent of the time or less. Trading systems which are correct 60 to 75 percent of the time are fairly rare, and those which are correct 70 percent of the time or more are extremely rare (assuming a reasonably large data sample). The lengthier the historical test, the less accurate the results. Statistically, this is called *regression to the mean.* Putting it in plain old-fashioned English, *most trading systems don't work.* And again, in plain old-fashioned English, trading systems which have the principles of risk management built into them increase the odds of success dramatically.

The random walk hypothesis as proposed by Malkiel in his classic book *A Random Walk Down Wall Street* (Norton, New York, 1973) poses a particularly cogent argument in opposition to system development. Malkiel's thesis is that *the vast majority of market behavior is random, and, hence, attempts to predict prices are essentially useless and moreover unprofitable.* Although I don't fully agree with everything Malkiel has said in his classic book, I do believe that he has made some good points. I have long felt that traders who can consistently follow a rational, unoptimized method of trading and who can, at the same time, employ strict principles of risk management can achieve profitable results, possibly equal to or greater than the results which may be achieved by rigid trading system followers. The essence of any trading system is not the system itself but rather its approach to risk management and the skill of the trader implementing that system.

What's Left?

Am I telling you, therefore, that you ought not to trade according to a system? Am I saying that there are no trading systems which are worth trading? Am I saying that trading systems should not be tested or developed? Or do I wish to lead you in an entirely different direction? Frankly, I'm telling you that your time is more efficiently spent on developing your own methods of risk management and trading style as opposed to optimizing trading systems. You will find within this book few examples of trading system results, no outrageous claims, and furthermore, repeated warnings about the limitations of trading systems. This book will *not* present you with a stable of optimized, perfected, and curve-fitting trading systems which look great on paper but which will not perform well for you in the future. System development and system testing are illusory. Do not depend upon them too much—they will lead you astray.

Accordingly, I feel that serious day traders and in fact serious traders regardless of their time-frame orientation should devote their energies to the following:

1. *Research and develop timing tools* which have shown relatively high accuracy as opposed to trading systems per se.

2. *Focus on methods of risk management* including limitation of losses, maximization of profits, and such important issues as the use of trailing stop losses.

3. *Focus on improving your relationship with the markets and develop your skills as a trader,* skills which will serve you well regardless of whether you are using a trading system which has been thoroughly back-tested or not.

Markets Change—Market Participants Change

Another very important consideration in the use of trading systems and in trading system development is the fact that the characteristics of markets change. The markets of today are distinctly different from the markets of the 1950s, the 1960s, the 1970s, and the 1980s. Each era of market activity has had its own characteristic issues, and each market has experienced significant fundamental developments which have changed its tone and underlying response styles.

Furthermore, the nature of the players has changed. Whereas institutions were involved only marginally in futures trading until the early 1980s, they now constitute a major force in the markets; their collective buying and selling can produce significant market volatility. A trading system, therefore, which would have worked well in the 1970s may not work well in the 1990s. This is why trading systems show regression to the mean the farther back they are tested. You may wish to try a little experiment on your own. Develop a trading system based on the last 5 years' worth of price data. Once it has been developed, test that same trading system on the last 10 years' worth of data. In all probability, you'll find that the system has diminished in its performance. Now, test the last 15 years of data. Result? You'll find in a vast majority of cases that the system was even less effective. This is a classic example of regression to the mean. It shows that markets change their characteristics and that the players in a market change as well. This in turn affects the ability of trading systems to show consistent performance over time.

Striving for Solutions

What are the answers to the significant questions and limitations I've posed regarding trading system development and back testing? There are several potentially valid answers. First and foremost, trading system research should be given less attention rather than more attention. I do not believe that the ultimate trading system using conventional methods of research will ever be uncovered or revealed. I feel very strongly that the emphasis must be the development of simple but repetitive and reliable market relationships as opposed to systems per se. Second, the day trader must develop specific methods for implementing consistent intraday market relationships within the context of effective risk management. And third, the day trader (in fact, all traders) must be sensitive to changing market conditions. Monitor your performance closely in order to determine when conditions are changing and when you ought to respond by changing your trading style and methods. This book is about these solutions.

The Role of Artificial Intelligence

There is one potentially significant exception to everything I've said above. Computer software and hardware technology are now advancing at such a rapid pace that the development of artificial-intelligence-based trading systems will, I feel, in the very near future, become a significant force in the marketplace. I refer here specifically to systems based on neural networks. Until recently, the computer hardware and software required to mimic the functioning of the human brain were extremely costly and, in many cases unavailable other than to government and large industry. However, with the advent of affordable computer memory as well as faster computer chip speeds, the ability to analyze vast amounts of data on many levels simultaneously has opened the door to many new and powerful possibilities in the field of artificial intelligence. Artificial intelligence is the terminology used to describe machine-based or computer-simulated intelligence which attempts to simulate the human problem-solving process. Applications of this new technology are already being used in science, business, and industry, particularly in the area of industrial robotics.

A sophisticated branch of artificial intelligence, termed *neural networks*, actually models its software on theories of human thinking, attempting thereby to replicate the human learning process and moreover to create a computer program which learns from its errors and which performs better with more experience. Although both these goals are certainly lofty, they are not unrealistic in terms of current and anticipated technology. Because neural networks seek to mimic the intellectual processes of the human brain, this new technology promises to spawn a vast new area of trading methodology, one which is based on computer-learning models. If the promise of the neural networks in the area of stock and futures trading turns out to be as significant as I think it will, then this new technology could very well change system development dramatically.

Because each neural analysis program is distinct in terms of the market forces it examines and the learning model it employs, very few neural programs will reach the same conclusions at the same time. Hence, neural analysis also promises a multiplicity of approaches which, in the final analysis, would be considered an extremely positive factor for the markets, since the players would not all be playing from the same side at the same time or from similar timing frames. Because of how neural analysis reaches its conclusions, the focus is primarily on pattern recognition and evaluation of current relationships which appear to be driving the markets. Since forces underlying market trends change from day to day and week to week, neural analysis programs which are sensitive to such changes will also change. Neural systems are dynamic; they are not subject to the static limitations of traditional trading systems. This, of course, promises to eliminate one of the major objections to traditional trading systems, which is that they are not responsive to underlying market conditions which can change dramatically over time.

Finally, neural analysis programs evaluate market inputs as do traditional trading systems. However, neural analysis programs can evaluate a vast number of inputs (by inputs I mean indicators), analyzing the combination of indicators which are driving market prices at any given time. Neural programs can combine the evaluation of technical as well as fundamental inputs concomitantly. In this way, neural analysis programs represent a quantum leap, possibly a several-quanta leap, from traditional systems. You'll be hearing much more about these new systems in the next few years.

Implications for the Future

Inasmuch as neural analysis programs could very well replace traditional trading methodologies during the next several years, the question naturally arises "why learn what's contained in this book or for that matter in any other system related or indicator related book?" The answer is simple indeed. As you have realized by now, my emphasis is not on system and not on technique per se, but rather on the development of trader skills. *Skill is what ultimately separates winners from losers.* The most effective trading system in the hands of an unskilled, undisciplined impulsive trader is a tool of destruction.

Conversely, a mediocre trading system with a knowledgeable, experienced, disciplined, and well-heeled trader at the helm can be a vehicle which affords vast wealth. Therefore, the skills which you will learn in this book (provided you are attentive and self-directed) will serve you well in the future regardless of the trading methodologies you choose to employ. Furthermore, the skills you learn in this book can be used as intellectual inputs for a neural computer brain which, when combined with other inputs can yield outstanding results. Hence, your time and money will lead to positive results regardless of what hot new systems make their debut. But enough for theory—now on to practice!

4
Day Trading with Moving Averages

Certain assumptions are made throughout this book regarding the expertise of my readers. Possibly these assumptions are too optimistic. Nevertheless, I will assume that, since you have purchased a book on day trading, you have already acquired some degree of sophistication and knowledge about the futures markets. I will, therefore, dispense with basic definitions in many cases, assuming that you are already familiar with the standard trading terminology. From time to time, however, I may choose to insult your intelligence by explaining simple concepts, knowing full well that you already have developed your own understanding of them. My purpose in doing so is to rectify what I feel is, at times, an erroneous understanding of these concepts. In addition, I may wish to redefine some terms within the day-trading context.

Moving Average Basics

Of all systems available to traders in the futures and stock markets, the vast majority are based on moving averages, or on a variation of the moving average theme. Moving averages are not difficult to understand, relatively simple to apply, and frequently quite easy to calculate. There are many different types of moving averages. Here is a brief list of the moving averages I've worked with, followed by a brief definition:

1. Simple Moving Average (MA). This is a moving average in which each price of the data series is assigned the same weight or value.

A 10-period moving average is calculated simply by summing all 10 values and dividing by 10. The second moving average value is calculated by dropping the first raw value from the sum and adding the eleventh value to the sum. This leaves a window of 10 data points which are then added and divided by 10. The result is a second value in the moving average series. The process continues with the next raw data point. A moving average of x time units in length always has x data points. When I refer to a 10-period moving average, I mean specifically 10 days, 10 hours, 10 years, 10 months, or 10 segments of 5 minutes each. The time length of the unit is referred to as the *period.*

Typically in our work with intraday moving averages, we will be dealing with moving averages of from one minute to one hour in length as the period. Consequently, if I refer to a 10-period simple moving average on the one minute data, I am referring to a moving average calculated by adding together the most recent ten one minute prices and dividing by ten. If I refer to a ten hour moving average I am referring to the last ten hours worth of prices (one price per hour), added together, and divided by ten.

2.   Exponential Moving Average (EMA).   An exponential moving average is calculated slightly differently than is a simple moving average inasmuch as it exponentially weights each value. The purpose of using an exponential moving average is, theoretically, to provide an average which will be more responsive, theoretically, to the underlying data. There are numerous sources which you may consult for the specifics of exponential MA calculation.

3.   Weighted Moving Average (WMA).   This is one of my favorite moving averages, because *it does not assign equal weight to all values in the data series.* There are two types of weighted moving averages, *front-weighted* (also called *front-loaded*), and *back-weighted* (also called *back-loaded*). If we refer to the front portion of the data as the most recent data, then a front-weighted moving average multiplies each value toward the most recent data by a constant weight or value in order to provide for greater impact of current data. A back-weighted moving average weights the earliest data in the price series in order to give it more significance in the final analysis.

4.   Smoothed Moving Average (SMA).   A smoothed moving average is a weighted moving average of a different type. In this case, the data is "smoothed" mathematically to keep the averages from moving around too much. This, it is hoped, will yield more stable signals.

5. Triangular Moving Average (TMA). Yet another type of moving average, the TMA is weighted to emphasize the normal statistical distribution. In other words, the extremes of the TMA are less heavily weighted than is the central portion of the TMA. This results in the TMA being more centered and, therefore, more responsive to the normal distribution qualities of the data series. In order to calculate a 7-day TMA, for example, the following procedure would be used:

Raw data: A, B, C, D, E, F, G (7 days)

Step 1:

$$x = (1 \times A) + (2 \times B) + (3 \times C) + (4 \times D) + (3 \times E) + (2 \times F) + (1 \times G)$$

Step 2:

$$\text{TMA} = x/16$$

(16 = sum of all multipliers)

Traditional Moving Average Systems: Assets and Liabilities

Moving averages have been used with varying degrees of success by stock and futures traders for many years. Although there are literally hundreds of possible variations on the theme of moving averages, the fact is that moving-average-based trading systems, regardless of their specific type, have some distinct limitations and only a few advantages.

Moving-average systems are trend-following systems. They get traders on board once a move has started based on the averages, and they either exit positions (i.e., "go flat") when a move has ended or reversed. MAs perform well when markets are in trends. However, in trendless or sideways markets, moving averages experience their greatest limitations and downfall. Since markets are in strong trends perhaps only 30 percent of the time, you'll find that most moving-average-based systems are accurate (i.e., correct) between 20 and 50 percent of the time. This relatively low accuracy rate, however, does *not mean* that MA-based systems cannot make money. They can, provided the essential rules of risk management and good trading are carefully followed. Before I discuss these, however, I'll give you some of the pros and cons of MAs.

As previously stated, the problem with moving-average-based systems is that they are not very accurate. Moving averages are lagging indicators. A *lagging indicator,* as its name suggests, is an indicator which follows the market and which, by its very nature, does not change direction until *after the market has changed direction.* The positive aspect of such indicators is that they frequently do not change direction until a new trend is under way.

The downside, is, of course, that what the moving-average perceives to be the start of a new trend may actually prove to be a very brief trend or it may be nothing more than a random variation or "hiccough" within the existing trend. But most moving-average systems aren't smart enough to distinguish between a real trend or a brief variation within the existing trend. Hence, they generate many false signals. Moving averages are basically deaf, blind, and dumb indicators. They say to the market, "lead me and I will follow." Provided the market establishes a meaningful trend, moving averages will do well. Yet, in the absence of a meaningful trend, or in a whipsaw type market, moving averages will suffer terribly, taking loss after loss after loss.

Another severe limitation of moving averages is the fact that in order to immunize them from false turns, they must necessarily sacrifice sensitivity. It is not, therefore, uncommon for a considerable amount of profit to be given back in awaiting an MA signal to exit an existing position. Similarly, new positions will often be entered well after a trend has changed, therefore, also sacrificing a good deal of the potential profit. Although there are some ways to minimize this problem period, it is, nevertheless, a serious one.

Yet another significant problem with moving-average-based systems which arises from the two foregoing limitations is that the systems are frequently incorrect. Most moving-average systems are correct between 20 and 40 percent of the time, with the upper end of this range being the exception rather than the rule. Yet, in spite of these limitations, moving-average-based systems continue to be very popular among technical traders and in particular, among fund managers. Why? There are several reasons: *First,* the use of moving averages requires very little in the way of sophisticated mathematics. Basic moving averages can be readily computed without the assistance of a computer and can be determined quickly, both on a daily as well as on an intraday basis. *Second,* moving-average-based systems provide specific trading signals which are a function of moving averages and/or prices crossing above or below one another. This is ideal for the strictly mechanical trader. *Third,* moving average systems in most cases are always-in-the-market systems. This means that with few exceptions, these systems go from long to short and short to long and rarely maintain a neutral position. The idea of always having a position in the market appeals to many traders who know that some of the most spectacular and potentially profitable market movements occur when traders do not have positions. *Fourth,* many traders fear that by not having a position, they take the risk of not being able to establish one at a reasonable entry price once a major price move has started. (Of course, commodity fund managers who share in the commission income of their funds love MA systems which trade frequently. After all, they can't help but have a vested interest if they participate in the commissions.) Yet a *fifth* reason for the popularity of moving averages is found in their simplicity. Moving averages do not require a great deal of understanding about the markets, yet they offer the attraction of a mathematical model which rings the bell of money managers who have a public image to maintain.

Because moving averages are so amenable to quick calculation, and because the signals derived from moving averages are so precise (do not confuse precise with accurate), they lend themselves readily to application for short-term and day trading.

This chapter will focus on a number of specific moving average applications which day traders may use, frequently with considerable success, provided they follow certain very basic rules of application. Although some of the methods are traditional, you will find some new and interesting ideas in what follows.

Moving Average Crossovers—Price versus MA

One of the most traditional and time-tested methods of moving-average application is the price-cross-above-MA method. The relationship is a very simple one indeed.

> **As long as price is above the MA, trend is defined as up**
> **As long as price is below the MA, trend is defined as down**

When price has been below the MA and then crosses above the MA, the trend changes from down to up. When price has been above the MA and then crosses below the MA, the trend changes from up to down. Figure 4-1 illustrates the basic relationships using a 9-period simple MA on a 30-minute T-bond futures chart. Note my comments.

Day traders may use price/MA relationships and crossovers to generate buy-and-sell signals as indicated in my illustration. As an aside, please note that my comments here are offered within the constraints of

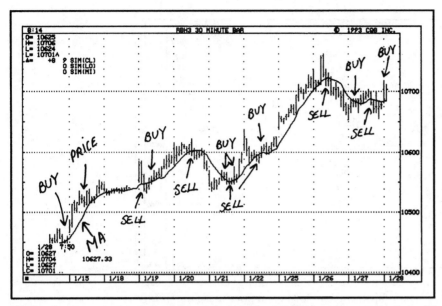

Figure 4-1. The basic relationships between the MA and price using a 9-period simple MA on a 30-minute T-bond futures chart.

the limitations I have previously given you about the use of moving averages. The simple rules are:

Buy when price closes above the MA after having been below it.

Sell when price has been below the MA after having been above it.

Using these rules yields many false signals, generates considerable commissions, and in the long run (or short run in this case) results in more heat than light.

There are two ways to overcome the above problem. First, adjust or fit the length of the MA to the market, and, second, determine which time frame is best. Here are some of my suggestions.

1. Length of the MA

Typically, the length of the moving average should be adjusted to accommodate the characteristics of the market which is being traded. In some cases, a slower MA serves the purpose better than a faster MA. Figure 4-2 shows the same market as Figure 4-1 but with an 18-period MA.

As you can see, the results are much, much better. And Figure 4-3 illustrates the same MA, 18 periods of 30-minute data on Swiss franc futures. Note my comments on each chart. You can see that buy signals occur when the closing price for each price bar has crossed above the

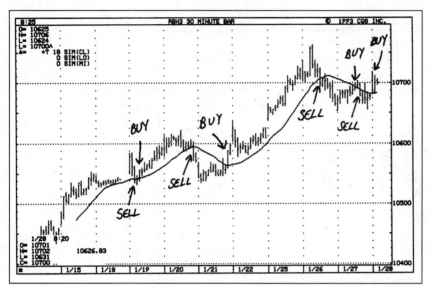

Figure 4-2. The basic relationships between the MA and price using an 18-period simple MA on a 30-minute T-bond futures chart.

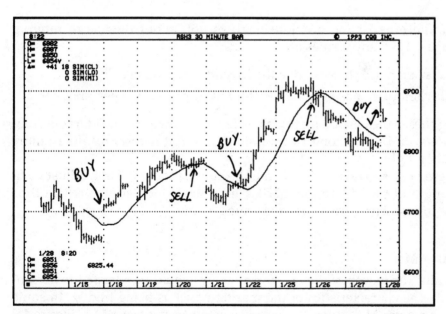

Figure 4-3. The basic relationships between the MA and price using an 18-period simple MA on a 30-minute Swiss franc futures chart.

moving-average price, which is the solid line. Conversely, sell signals occur when the closing price for a given price bar falls below the MA value. The relationships are extremely simple and mechanically applied.

2. Time Frame

The best time frames for a day trader are from 1 minute to 30 minutes. I can tell you from personal experience that if you want to go crazy you'll use a 1-minute time frame for trading. If, however, you want to retain some degree of sanity and order in your life you'll use a 5-minute time frame at the shortest. Many traders swear by the 3-minute charts in Standard & Poor's (S&P). I think this has merit as well. You will, however, have to decide what you want to do with your time. Trading by 3-minute charts, even by 5-minute charts, will require you to be "glued" to your price quotations. Most of the methods and techniques I'll discuss in this book will be applicable to time frames ranging from 5 to 30 minutes.

Evaluation of the MA Crossovers—
Price versus MA as a System

Although this approach is certainly simple enough and easily applied to virtually any market, it is not a good system to use in markets which are not trending. It is essentially a method which will lose you money between slippage and commission. Although the rules of entry and exit are specific and objective, using this method profitably is more of an art than a science. The overall accuracy of this technique is about 25 to 35 percent at best. If you are using this method on 30-minute to 60-minute data, strictly according to the rules outlined above, then an MA length of about 10 to 14 units is best. The results, after slippage and commission, however, in most markets will be less than $100 per trade. I suggest you stay away from this method. It will only cost you time and money.

Dual MA Crossover

One way to limit the number of false signals from MA systems is to use two MAs as opposed to one. In this case the rules of application are also very simple. Typically, the two MAs used are related on about an 8 to 1 ratio. In other words, if we were using a 3-period MA of the 5-minute closing prices for our first MA, then we would use about a 24-period MA of the closing price for our second MA. This would give us the desired ratio. Do note that in some applications of MAs (to be discussed later) these ratios do not apply. Figure 4-4 shows the basic buy-and-sell signals on a 30-minute T-bond futures chart.

The purpose of using two MAs is to slow the response time required for a crossover. This slowing, although beneficial because it generates fewer false signals, is also detrimental in that it requires a slower response time by the moving averages and thereby signals market entries and exits less responsively. It is, therefore, very important to select the correct combination of MA lengths, a combination which strikes the proper balance of response time and minimization of false crossovers.

Although the application of two MAs seems to offer more profit potential and fewer false signals than does the price-versus-MA crossover, this approach is not one of the better ones, since it is subject to the limitations of all lagging market indicators. As a point of information, note the performance history test results in Figure 4-5 for the dual MA crossover system in S&P futures.

As you can see from the accompanying historical performance summary (Figure 4-5), the dual MA crossover system is not impressive. Note that the results reflect carrying positions overnight. By closing out positions at the end of the day the performance of this method deteriorates into a losing proposition. Hence, I urge you to stay away from it for the purpose of day trading. In S&P futures this method is an overall loser.

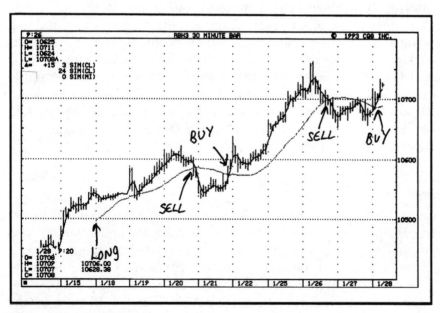

Figure 4-4. Basic dual MA (3 and 24 periods) and buy-and-sell signals on a 30-minute T-bond futures chart.

MovAvg Crossover SP E92-30 min 01/02/92–12/31/92

Performance Summary: All Trades

Total net profit	$20325.00	Open position P/L	$0.00
Gross profit	$49025.00	Gross loss	$−28700.00
Total number of trades	137	Percent profitable	55
Number winning trades	76	Number losing trades	61
Largest winning trade	$2550.00	Largest losing trade	$−800.00
Average winning trade	$645.07	Average losing trade	$−470.49
Ratio average win/average loss	1.37	Average trade (win & loss)	$148.36
Maximum consec. winners	9	Maximum consec. losers	4
Average bars in winners	6	Average bars in losers	5
Maximum intraday drawdown	$−3400.00		
Profit factor	1.71	Maximum contracts held	1
Account size required	$6400.00	Percent return on account	318

The performance summary above is based on the following assumptions:

3- versus 54-period moving average

30-minute S&P futures

1/2/92–12/31/92

$800 stop loss

No deduction for slippage and commission

Positions exited at the end of the trading session

Figure 4-5. Results of the dual MA crossover system in S&P futures. *(Reprinted with permission of Omega Research Inc.)*

Moving Averages as Support and Resistance

Another approach to the use of MAs is to use them as measures of support and resistance. Generally defined, *support* is a price level from which the market is expected to recover should it decline following a price rally. *Resistance* is a price level from which the market will decline following rallies in a declining trend. Support is used for the purpose of establishing long positions on price reactions or corrections during rising markets. Resistance is the price level used to establish positions on rallies during bear trends.

Throughout the history of the stock and futures markets, there have been many efforts to specifically define support and resistance levels or areas. Each school of market analysis has developed its own methodology. Chartists point to certain formations, trend lines, and price-versus-volume patterns as their preferred methods of establishing technical support and resistance levels.

Point and figure chartists have their unique methodology as well. And, of course, those who adhere to the teachings of Gann and Elliott use percentage retracements and Gann angles as their preferred methods of establishing support and resistance. While I do not discount the validity or potential of such methods, I find them too intricate. I have developed my own approach which has served me well during the years. The sections which follow illustrate some of these ideas and techniques.

Dual MA Crossover for Support and Resistance

This approach is a very viable one for day traders, and I recommend it strongly. Its assets are clearly that it provides a specific entry point either long or short and that it is relatively simple to use. Its downside is that it is not an entirely objective or strictly mechanical methodology.

Applications of Intraday MA for Support and Resistance Trading

The application of this approach is very simple indeed. There are basically three steps involved:

- *Use the dual MA crossover method.* The 8:1 ratio suggested earlier should be used.

- *Determine market trend.* This is accomplished by examining the price chart for the last crossover signal. If the last crossover signal was a bullish signal, then the trend is assumed to be up. If the last crossover was a bearish signal, then the trend is assumed to be down. Please consult Figures 4-6 and 4-7 for specifics.

- *Buy on price declines to the longer of the two MAs which serves as support and sell short if the trend is down on price rallies to the longer of the two MA lines.* Again, please consult Figures 4-6 and 4-7 for specific illustrations of this approach. In any case, you will close your position, win, lose, or draw, by the end of the trading session.

Since there is no way to determine whether a decline to the MA line in a bullish market is the start of a new trend down or just a reaction on which to buy, you will need to protect your position with a stop loss.

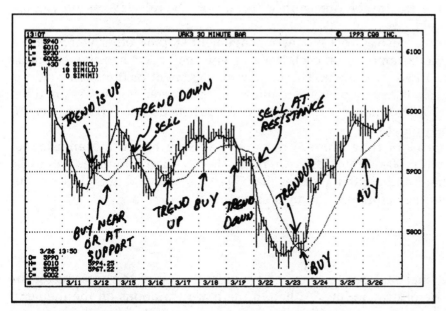

Figure 4-6. Dual MA crossover signals with support and resistance.

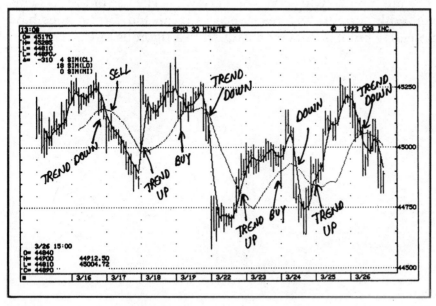

Figure 4-7. Dual MA crossover signals using support and resistance.

Stop losses may be determined in any of several ways as previously discussed.

You may use a strict money management stop, in other words, risk a fixed dollar amount on each trade or you may use a specific technique for stop loss placement. The money management or dollar risk stop is self-explanatory; however, I remind you that larger stop losses are often preferable to smaller stop losses, since markets do need room to negotiate their moves.

In terms of time frame, I recommend using between 5-minute, 10-minute, or 30-minute data. Anything shorter than 5 minutes would be too short, and anything longer than 30 minutes would not allow for sufficient time before the trading session ends.

In Summary

In the final analysis, I recommend against the use of MA systems for the purpose of day trading. Although there are variations on the theme of moving average (to be discussed), the vast majority of methods do not yield much more than losses and commissions. Avoid these systems since they are not likely to serve you very well. The use of MA systems, however, with support and resistance as trend indicators, does have good potential, but it is difficult to subject to a rigorous test.

5

Intraday Application
of Stochastics

The application of the stochastic indicator (SI) as originally developed by George Lane offers considerable potential for day traders as well as position traders. Those who are familiar with the immediate action signals which were presented in the *Stochastic Fantastic* book co-authored by Mark Silber and myself are aware of how the SI may be valuable both in position trading as well as in short-term trading.[*] The immediate action signals are also likely to be applicable in the day-trading time frame; however, they have not yet been fully tested.

This chapter will illustrate some basic applications of stochastics for the purpose of day trading and will provide some guidelines regarding SI application and applications, possible limitations, advantages, and expectations.

Explaining Stochastics Quickly and Simply

As many of you already know, the stochastic indicator consists of two values, percent K and percent D. Percent D is a derivative of percent K. Percent K is derived itself from the fast stochastic indicator which is derived using a simple mathematical formula. We will be working with the slow stochastic indicator, so termed because it is a moving average of the fast stochastic indicator and, therefore, makes slower oscillations. It is well known that stochastics can be used in many different ways.

[*]J. Bernstein and M.A. Silber, *Stochastic Fantastic*, MBH, P.O. Box 353, Winnetka, Ill. 60093, 1992.

Sometimes I feel that there are as many different applications of SI as there are futures traders; SI is one of the most popular contemporary indicators in the futures markets. *This, in and of itself, does not mean that SI is the best indicator.* On the contrary, it may very well mean that as commonly used SI may be one of the worst indicators. Although I do not believe that this is true, I am by nature a contrarian. When applied consistently and with concise trading rules, the SI in its traditional applications can be a profitable indicator for day traders (and others as well). Here is a synopsis of the basic stochastic indicator followed by some of the more traditional applications for day traders and then by my stochastic pop (SP) method which is, I feel, one of the more effective methods of day trading.

The Basic Stochastic Indicator

Futures traders have discovered through trial and error (mostly through error) that effective timing indicators can be applied in many ways and in a variety of combinations with other indicators. Dr. George Lane advanced numerous applications for his stochastic indicator; I have, through persistence, considerable research, and the "school of hard knocks" amplified on George Lane's original research. In fact, George has adapted at least one of my uses of stochastics, the stochastic pop indicator, to his own use.

Simply stated, the SI is a price oscillator which compares today's price behavior with the behavior of prices x number of periods ago. A 14-day SI, for example, compares a derivative of today's price with price 14 trading days ago. The raw stochastic number is converted to a percentage reading, smoothed, and then compared to a moving average of itself. Hence, the SI consists of two numbers expressed as percent at each price bar. Since both lines are smoothed, and since one line, percent D is a derivative of percent K (usually a 3-period moving average of the first-line percent K) the visual effect is one which easily shows highs and lows in the SI correlated closely with highs and lows in price.

There are two forms of the SI, fast and slow. The fast SI consists of two lines which often gyrate wildly from low to high and back again, and the slow SI is a smoothed version of fast and moves more gradually from low to high and back again. There is a strong correlation between tops and bottoms in price and SI tops and bottoms. The SI is, therefore, a powerful indicator which may be used by short-term, position, and day traders alike.

The important issue regarding the SI, whether fast or slow and whether 9-period or 25-period, is its method of application. As we will see later on there are numerous ways in which SI may be used. It is the purpose of this chapter to provide you with what I feel are some of the most powerful methods for day traders. I am confident that those who understand and consistently apply the principles we are about to teach will appreciate both the simplicity and power of our techniques.

Before introducing the basic approaches to SI timing I'd like to stress the following important aspects of stochastics:

1. Many traders consider an SI of 75 percent or higher as an indication that a top is imminent, and a stochastic of 25 percent or lower is often considered an imminent sign of a bottom.

2. The fact that the SI reaches an overbought condition (i.e., 75 percent or higher) or an oversold condition (25 percent or lower) does not necessarily indicate that action should be taken immediately. This is the single most severe drawback of traditional stochastic implementation.

3. The SI is used by many traders as a stand-alone system. Although there is nothing wrong with this approach, I have found that with only a few exceptions the addition of timing indicators can improve overall results, regardless of which SI technique you are using.

Basic Approaches to SI Timing

1. Percent *K* and Percent D
Crossover Signals

The SI (stochastic indicator) can be used in either its fast or slow mode. The slow SI mode is a moving average version of the fast SI mode. We recommend using slow SI, since fast SI oscillates too wildly. One method of SI timing is to use the slow SI for buy and sell signals on crossovers of the percent *K* and percent *D* SI lines. This approach is illustrated in Figure 5-1. This application of SI requires a considerable amount of trading, trading which varies directly with the length of the SI indicator. Shorter lengths of SI result in more trades and vice versa. This technique is subject to the same limitations found in virtually all moving average and oscillator applications—it generates numerous false signals and tends to give back too much in profits.

2. 25 Percent and 75 Percent SI
Crossovers

Generally speaking an SI reading of 75 percent or higher is considered overbought and a reading of 25 percent or lower is considered oversold.

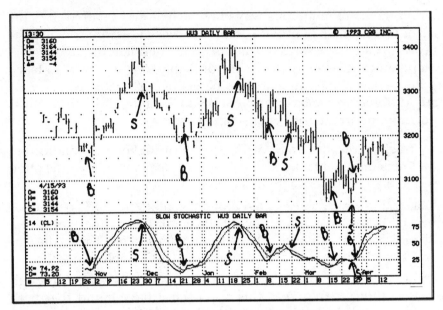

Figure 5-1. SI buy-and-sell signals on percent *K* and percent *D* crossovers.

Because the SI can remain in the overbought (OB) or oversold (OS) area for lengthy periods we advise against sell decisions made simply on the basis of an OB condition or buy decisions made simply on the basis of an OS condition. If you use the SI for the purpose of selling and buying on such extremes, you must wait for the cross to occur from OB back under 75 or for a cross above 25 from OS. This approach to the use of SI requires you to wait for SI to rise to 75 percent or higher and then to fall below 75 percent on a closing basis; when it does you will sell or reverse your long position to short. Wait for SI to fall to 25 percent or lower and then to rise above 25 percent on a closing basis. When it does you will buy or reverse your short position to the long side. This application of SI has good potential for trading in virtually all time frames.

Remember, however, that the SI alone will not tell you where to put your stop or where to take your profit. You must use your other methods to do so or you must rely on your own judgment for stop-loss placement. As with any method or system you must be prepared to take your losses when necessary.

Please don't resort to excuses to avoid taking your loss and don't add to losing positions just because the SI is heading in a given direction. The SI is not infallible. I have found, however, that when used in conjunction with the other timing signals, SI achieves a greater degree of accuracy while limiting false signals and risk.

I have found the 75/25 approach to be more fruitful than the cross-over method described in the previous section. The technique is very simple. Figures 5-2 and 5-3 illustrate this approach using 5- and 10-minute data. The 75/25 method may be used in virtually any time frame and will work well in 5-, 10-, or 15-minute charts. It is also applicable to 30-minute data; however, when used on data longer than 20 minutes' duration, it no longer serves the purposes of day traders very well.

Intraday Stochastic Pop: Definition

I've been asked on many occasions why I call my unique use of stochastics the "stochastic pop" indicator (referred to hereinafter as SP). Very simply, the SP is so termed because *it enters markets when most traders consider markets to be overbought or oversold.* In other words, the SP signals a buy when a market is considered by the vast majority of traders to be overbought and incapable of going any higher. SP enters short positions when the majority of traders considers the market to be oversold and unlikely to go any lower. In other words, *I have found that markets tend to POP like a kernel of corn at the right temperature, once they reach certain levels on the SI.*

Through the years I have found that the ideas of overbought and oversold are fallacies. *The fact is that a market is never too overbought to go*

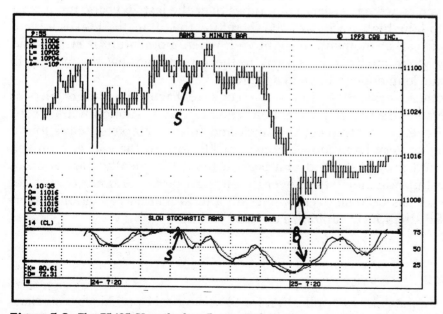

Figure 5-2. The 75/25 SI method on 5-minute data.

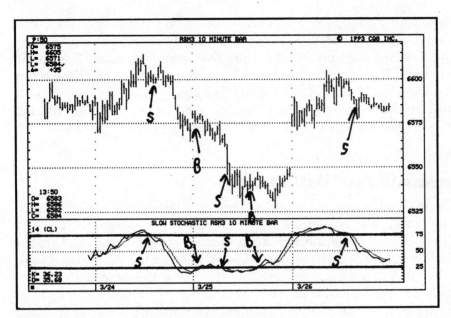

Figure 5-3. The 75/25 SI method on 10-minute data.

higher and hardly ever too oversold to go lower. Since there is a natural limit as to how low prices can go (i.e., zero), there does eventually come a point at which prices are ideally too low and oversold. On the upside, however, as we have seen many times over the last 25 years, there is no limit to how high prices can go. Therefore, the SP method takes advantage of market momentum by buying when momentum is strong and selling when momentum is weak in the expectation that the move will continue long enough to yield a profit.

In other words, SP is, in a sense, consistent with the laws of physics which state that a body in motion tends to stay in motion until it runs out of energy. In studying the stock and futures markets I have found that many very large moves occur quickly toward the end of a bullish trend and toward the end of a bearish trend. Frequently, the period of greatest upside momentum over the shortest period of time occurs after a market has become overbought and after a market has become oversold. SP attempts to capitalize on this condition.

SP Parameters

Here are the rules of application for SP. Using a 14-period slow stochastic indicator, a buy signal will be triggered when percent *K* is at 75 percent or higher at the end of the period you are using. For the purpose of day trading with the SP, I prefer either 5- or 10-minute data. Consequently, once the SI has closed at 75 percent or higher on percent K using 5- or 10-minute data, you will be buying immediately upon that 5- or 10-minute posting. Your buy will always be at the market. From time to time there may be sufficient leeway to allow a specific price order; however, I leave that type of jockeying up to you, since it is not usually a simple matter. Once you have established your position, use either a risk management stop loss or exit your position at the market as soon as percent K and percent D have crossed one another at the end of your 5- or 10-minute segment.

See Figures 5-4, 5-5, and 5-6 for graphic explanations and illustrations of the SP method. Note that the following abbreviations are used on many of the charts in this chapter as well as in the chapters which follow:

B = buy to establish new long position

S = sell to establish new short position

SL = close out long position and go flat

CS = cover short position and go flat

F = forced out at end of day

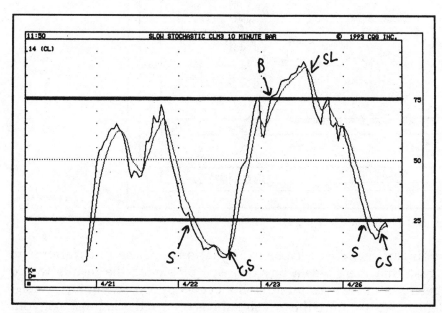

Figure 5-4. Ideal representation of the SP method.

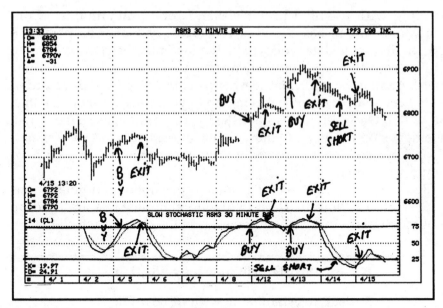

Figure 5-5. The SP method in real time, Swiss Franc.

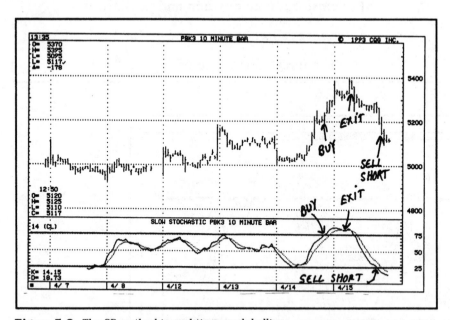

Figure 5-6. The SP method in real time, pork bellies.

As you can see from a close examination of these illustrations, in every case that there was a buy or a sell SP signal, the results would have been profitable even after having been stopped out on the exit signal. Remember that once the exit signal has occurred you must exit your position at the market.

Assume now that once you have entered by SP and exited according to the rules, percent *K* declines under 75 percent and then in a future at the end of a subsequent 5- or 10-minute segment goes to 75 percent or higher. What to do? Simply enter a long position again and trade by the rules. You will find a number of such instances illustrated in Figures 5-7 and 5-8.

Although the SP technique is ultimately very simple, it does require close attention, and you must, by all means, be there watching for those crossovers or you will lose money with this method. Before you attempt to implement this approach, take the time to follow it closely in actual market conditions so that you may test your knowledge and develop your skill with the SP method.

As you can see from the illustrations, the SP sell condition on an intraday basis also uses 5- or 10-minute data; however, it sells once percent *K* falls below 25 percent after first having been above it. Price execution is at the market in all cases, although as I've said earlier, you may decide to fool with specific price orders on your own if you'd like to take the chance. Exit of the SP sell will be at the market once percent *K* and percent *D* have crossed.

In any event, do remember that the SP intraday method is merely a day-trading method. I recommended against carrying positions beyond the end of the trading session. You must be out of your SP trade by the end of the day in order for it to qualify as a true day trade.

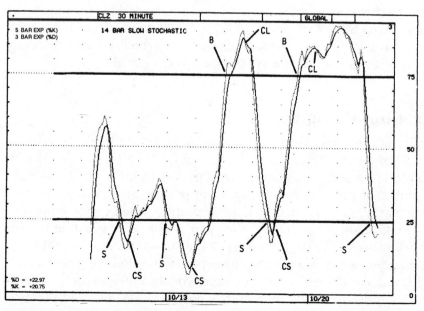

Figure 5-7. Ideal representation of the stochastic pop showing method—multiple signals.

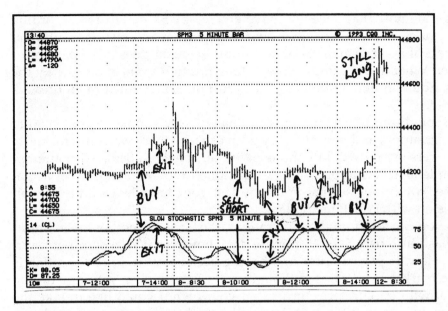

Figure 5-8. The SP method in real time—multiple signals.

Markets in Which SP Works Well

In my experience, SP on an intraday basis works well in highly volatile markets. Naturally, this includes most of the currencies, crude oil at times, S&P most of the time, and T-bonds at times. Perhaps SP's most consistent performance is in S&P futures. Since market characteristics will change over time, I urge you to watch the markets closely in order to allow the use of SP signals in other markets which are not currently active or volatile but which may become so in the future.

Hit-and-Run Trading Using the SP

One of the characteristics of the SP method is that it lends itself readily to the application of my "hit-and-run" technique. What this amounts to is simply entering a long or a short position consistent with the signals, staying with that position for a fairly brief period, and exiting the position at the market in order to grab a quick profit on the long or short side. The advantage here is, of course, that you will find it possible to take many quick profits. The disadvantage is that in so doing you will sacrifice larger moves which may occur once you have exited the position.

In order to have the best of all possible worlds, I suggest trading several units as opposed to one unit. Here's how it would work in practice. Assume that an SP buy signal has occurred. Instead of entering just one contract, you enter two or four, preferably in even units. As soon as the market has moved in your favor by a predetermined amount (100 points in S&P futures for example), you exit one unit. You hold the remaining unit long until the stochastic lines have crossed at the end of a 5- or 10-minute segment, which is where your ideal exit would have been. In so doing, you will trade one unit for hit and run, the other unit according to the rules.

Variation on the Theme of SP

Because markets can continue to run in their existing direction once an SP signal has occurred, I have developed yet another application of SP which is a more aggressive one. By aggressive, I mean one which tends to hold a position longer than the original SP application once the signal has occurred. Examine Figure 5-9. It illustrates a situation where an SP signal occurred subsequent to which a number of crossovers developed which would have caused you to exit your SP position according to the rules I gave you earlier. If, however, you did not exit when the percent *K* and percent *D* lines crossed but rather maintained your position, the potential profit would have been significantly greater. This is a more aggressive method because it allows you to hold your original SP position for a longer period of time. *To exit the position use a close trailing stop*

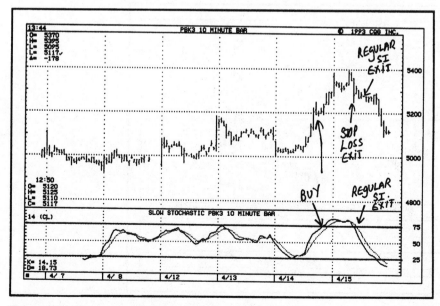

Figure 5-9. The aggressive SP technique, pork bellies.

*which will follow up your position preferably every half hour or more frequent-
ly in order to lock in your profit and protect you in the event of a quick reversal
in trend.*

A good illustration is provided in Figure 5-10, which depicts an SP
signal followed by a continued uptrend, an exit indication on the original SP method, but a maintenance of the long position beyond the original SP exit with a detailed follow-up stop procedure as suggested. See
also Figure 5-10 for similar illustrations of the aggressive SP technique.

As you can see, using this technique allows you, in most cases, to participate in the larger moves subsequent to an exit on the original SP
method. The aggressive SP technique is not recommended for conservative day traders, assuming that there is such a thing as a conservative
day trader. For those interested in the technique, I strongly recommend
following it closely for several weeks before deciding to pursue this
approach.

What You Can Expect

The SP technique has been tested extensively on historical data dating
back to the 1960s. Using various combinations of percentages to trigger
SP entry (i.e., 75 percent, 65 percent, 60 percent for buying; 25 percent,
15 percent, 30 percent for selling), I have found that the accuracy of SP

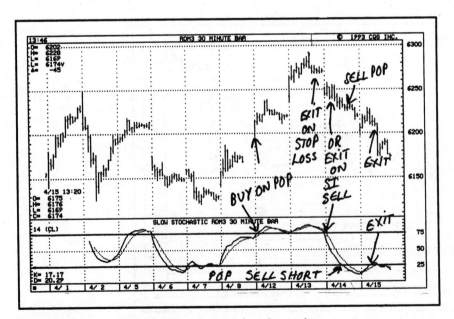

Figure 5-10. The aggressive SP technique, deutche mark.

in terms of follow-through is high. Even in a large sample size such as the one I tested, accuracies in terms of follow through in the direction of the signal as high as 65 percent were not uncommon during certain time frames. However, since the SP method both in its original form and in the aggressive mode is more of a method than a solid mechanical system, results in terms of application will vary from trader to trader. Although I will not guarantee definitive performance results since all traders trade differently, I can tell you that *if you use both the original SP and aggressive SP methods consistently and with close attention in terms of follow-up stops, you can do extremely well.*

Preferred Markets for SP Application

Although SP signals will occur in virtually every market, the day trader is looking specifically at those markets which have a high tick value and sufficient volatility to generate meaningful moves within the day time frame. The old standbys, S&P, Swiss franc, British pound, T-bonds, crude oil, heating oil, etc., should definitely be considered as day-trade candidates. However, there are other markets which, subsequent to major news items, reports, and other fundamentally inspired events can also yield outstanding day-trade pop opportunities. These should be considered as well. I refer specifically to such markets as cotton, lumber, pork bellies, and soy beans.

6
Gaps, Gaps, Gaps

Of all the short-term trading systems I've researched, traded with, and developed, my favorite ones are those which use opening price gaps as a methodology for entering trades. The reason I prefer systems based on gaps is primarily that *they require less attention than any other methods I know.* With the gap systems which I will discuss in this chapter, orders are entered either on the opening or 1 hour after the opening, and closed out either at a specific stop loss or on the close of trading. Naturally, for those traders who wish to follow the markets during the day this is certainly possible using the gap system; however, it is not necessary. Before discussing the gap systems, let's define what I mean by an *opening gap.* Surprising as it may seem, there are still many traders who do not understand the concept or the definition of an opening gap.

> **An opening gap occurs when today's opening price**
> **is either greater than yesterday's high price**
> **or less than yesterday's low price.**

Here's an example. Let's assume that yesterday's price range was $59.10 as the high, $58.60 as the low. If today's opening price is greater than $59.10, then an opening price gap UP has occurred. If, however, today's opening price is less than $58.60 which was yesterday's low, then an opening price gap *down* has occurred.

There has been some controversy as to what constitutes the opening price. This is an important consideration for day traders, so let me give you my definition of the opening price. If you are watching an on-line quotation system or if you consult your local newspaper or financial listings of futures prices, you will see that an opening price is usually indicated in the far left column. The prices read open, high, low, and close. Sometimes the *close* is referred to as a *settlement*. For our purposes, I define the *opening price* as the first print price.

Specifically, what I mean here is that the first price which appears on your screen is considered for the purposes of our discussion to be the opening price. I say this because frequently the exchange will define the opening price as slightly different than what the first print may be. Occasionally, a market opens in a range of prices. In other words, there will be no one specific opening price as defined by the exchange. Rather, there may be two or three opening prices, all of which occurred at the same time.

In such cases the exchange uses the range of the opening prices, selecting the midpoint as the opening price. This is not sufficient for our purposes. You must use the first print. In the vast majority of cases, the first print will not differ significantly, if at all, from the exchange-defined opening price. Figures 6-1 and 6-2 show the ideal gap open up and down signals. Gaps on actual charts are very easy to find and use if you know what you're looking for.

As you can see, it is very easy to identify an opening price gap due to its specific definition. This is why opening price gaps can be used objectively and as close to mechanically as possible.

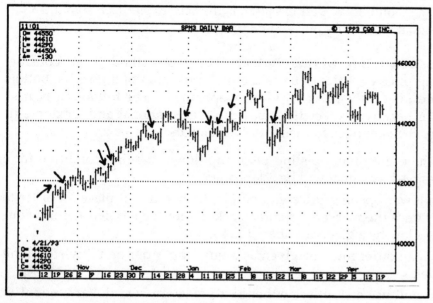

Figure 6-1. Opening price gap up.

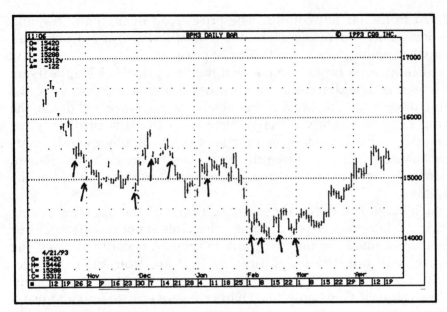

Figure 6-2. Opening price gap down.

Gap Trading Rules and Definitions

Gap Open Signals (GO)

I use two types of gap signals. The first is called the *gap open* (GO) signal. The second, to be defined later, is the *delayed gap open* signal (DGO). Each signal has its buy and sell parameters.

Gap Down Buy Signal Rules.   The gap methods I use consider opening price gaps down to be the first indication of a possible bottom and intraday rally. Most gap lower openings occur following bearish news or negative expectations based on international and/or domestic events. Here are rules for using the GO signals:

1. In the event of an opening price gap down, the first condition for a possible buy signal will be established.
2. If a lower opening price gap occurs, then you will place an order to buy once the market has come back up and penetrated the previous day's low by a given number of ticks.
3. Such an order must be given as a buy-stop-order or a buy-stop-limit order.
4. You will use a stop loss either at a predetermined dollar amount or several ticks below the day's low once your order has been filled.

5. Of the two stop methods, I prefer the money management dollar stop loss because, in many cases, the day's price range will have been too narrow to permit a reasonable stop loss to be placed.

Let me be specific about the buy condition which occurs after a gap lower opening. First, I'll begin with an example. This example refers to Figure 6-3. Assume that March S&P futures establish a daily trading range yesterday of 410.00 high, 408.00 low, and 408.50 close. A gap lower opening will establish the first condition for a possible GO buy signal. You know yesterday's high, low, and close (for this method knowing the close is not important). The market opens today at 407.50, 100 points lower than yesterday's close and 50 points lower than yesterday's low. *The first condition for a gap-buy-trade on a lower opening has been established.*

Due to the gap lower opening you would now enter a buy order by placing a buy stop or a buy-stop-limit, two ticks above the low of the previous day which would be 408.10 (408.00 + 0.10). What does this mean? This means that *if the market turns around and goes back up through the low of the previous day by two ticks, your buy stop will be elected and you will be long the market.* See Figure 6-3 for an illustration of this condition. In this intance the gap signal went long may cocoa as shaun and closed out the long position at the end of the day.

The rationale for this trade, both operationally and psychologically, is fairly understandable. If the market opens down price gap, the majority

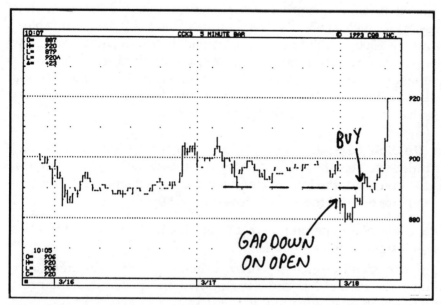

Figure 6-3. Gap down buy signal.

of traders interpret this to be a bearish sign, expecting prices to go lower. This brings in more selling. The market moves lower. If selling begins to "dry up" (that is, if the selling pressure decreases), then prices will not drop any further. If the market is strong enough to then rally back up through the low of the previous day, many traders will interpret this as a bullish indication and a negation of the lower opening price gap. Therefore, they begin to buy and prices will move higher. You will want to be in on the long side of such a move because *frequently such "surprise" rallies after lower opening price gaps tend to accentuate upside movement.*

Once you are long the market, at least two decisions need to be made. The first decision is where to put your stop loss. As you know, I have stressed the use of stop losses repeatedly and stress it here once again. Initially, your stop loss may be placed several ticks (most often two ticks) below the low of the day at the time that your buy order was filled. Therefore, if the low of the day was 399 and your buy stop was filled at 401.10, your stop loss would be placed two ticks below 399, or in this case, 398.90. Another procedure for stop losses is based strictly on risk management. In other words, a dollar amount stop will be used regardless of the low of the day. Typically, traders attempt to use very small dollar risk stop losses for day trading; however, I do not necessarily agree with this when it comes to such volatile markets as the currencies and S&P futures. My research has shown that larger stops are preferable. Unfortunately, this does not sit well with many traders who have limited amounts of capital to risk. I have found, for example, that a stop loss of as much as $2500 in S&P futures (500 points) is preferable to a stop loss of $500 or 100 points. Unfortunately, it is a sad but true fact that speculators have limited capital. Yet, the other side of the coin is that the larger your intraday stop loss, the greater the probability that you will remain in the trade and exit it profitably by the end of the day. This is what my intensive research has confirmed.

Gap Up Sell Signal.   Opening price gaps to the upside provide opportunities to sell the market short for a day trade. The procedure here is the inverse of the lower opening price gap which is used for buying. See Figure 6-4 and the rules below for specifics:

1. In the event of an opening price gap up, the first condition for a possible sell signal will be established.
2. If a higher opening price gap occurs, then you will place an order to sell once the market has come back down and penetrated the previous day's high by a given number of ticks.

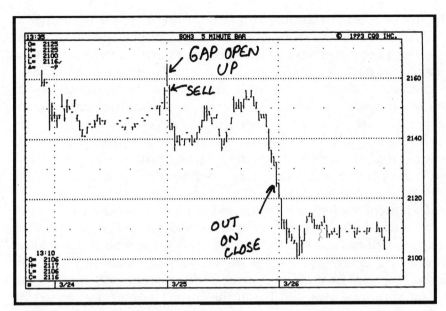

Figure 6-4. Gap up sell signal.

3. Such an order must be given as a sell stop order or a sell stop limit order.

4. You will use a stop loss either at a predetermined dollar amount or several ticks above the day's low once your order has been filled.

5. Of the two stop methods, I prefer the money management dollar stop loss because, in many cases, the day's price range will have been too narrow to permit a reasonable stop loss to be placed.

Assume the following situation: T-bond futures establish a trading range yesterday of 10201 as the low, 10214 as the high, 10203 as the close. Today, the market opens at 10126, a gap higher opening. This is a gap higher opening because the market has opened above the previous day's high price. In using the gap open lower and higher system for T-bond futures, I do not include the night session trading range. I am simply using the open, high, low, and close of the day session. You may want to use the system differently than I do; however, if you do, then I suggest you do some research with it before implementing these changes.

In this case, the gap higher opening establishes the first condition for a possible sell signal. A sell stop would be placed two ticks below the high of the previous day at 10212. You would not be able to use a sell-stop-limit because the Chicago Board of Trade, home of T-bond futures trading, does not accept stop limit orders.

If the market starts to decline and falls two ticks below the previous day's high, you would be stopped in to your short position. Your initial stop loss would be either several ticks above the then-current high of the day, or a money management dollar stop loss as discussed previously.

The psychology for the gap higher open sell is essentially similar to that of the gap lower open buy, only in reverse. When the market opens on a gap higher, those who are short rush to cover their positions and those who wish to get long, thinking the market is strong, support the higher opening. If, however, buying begins to diminish, prices will decline, falling through the gap and into yesterday's trading range by penetrating the previous day's high. This will be cause for concern to those who bought the higher opening and to those who exited short positions. Those who bought the higher opening and are concerned that a top has occurred will rush to sell their longs. And those who covered short positions on the opening will enter the market to reestablish their short positions. The combined selling of these two groups will force prices lower, and you hope you will be on the correct side of the market by being short. Naturally, both the gap lower buy trade and gap higher sell trade are closed out by the end of the trading session if the rules are being followed. See also Figures 6–8 through 6-11 for examples of gap trades.

Stop Losses and Follow-Up Stop Losses on Gap Trades. Frequently, gap lower or higher openings will produce fairly large moves within the day time frame. The professional day trader will want to maximize on these signals not only by having a specific stop loss but also *by attempting to lock in as much profit as possible so that in the long run overall risk exposure may be minimized.* I cannot overemphasize this last point. In order to do this I offer the following suggestions regarding stop losses and trailing stop losses:

- *When a gap signal trade has occurred,* make certain that once you are in a reasonably profitable position, *you place a stop loss to exit that position at your commission cost plus a small amount of profit so that if the market reverses course, you will have been stopped out without losing any money in most cases.* As far as follow-up stop losses are concerned I suggest that you develop your own procedure. In terms of dollar stop loss, a decision should be made on a per-market basis. In S&P futures for example, a 150 point or $750 lead on the market is a reasonable point at which to consider placing a stop loss at break-even plus commission or slightly higher. Remember that if you are "scalping" the market you will want to use an even closer follow-up stop loss.

- *Multiple units* or contracts may be considered as one way of maximizing your potential profit without significantly increasing your overall risk. Consider the following procedure: Rather than establish your initial position with one contract, you establish your initial position with two contracts. Assuming the market moves in your favor, you exit one contract at a predetermined target either determined technically or on a dollar basis while you *retain the remaining position with a specific break-even plus commission and small profit stop loss to protect you during the day and exit the position on the close or shortly before the close.* The multiple contract procedure combines, what I feel is the best of both situations, allowing you to have your profit and keep your trade as well.

■ *A trailing stop loss* may also be used. Although there is evidence to suggest that trailing stop losses for position trades do not work well, this is not necessarily true for day trades where the time length of a position is clearly finite. In the case of a runaway move in your favor, I suggest you follow up with either an hourly or a half-hourly stop using the last half hour low or high as your stop loss point. So, for example, if you have entered an S&P gap trade on the long side which then moves sharply in your favor and continues to move in your favor for a fairly extended period during the day, follow up that position by placing a stop loss below the low of the previous half hour or the previous hour if you prefer. In the case of a short position which has moved strongly in your favor, follow up by placing a stop loss above the high of the previous half hour or hour if you prefer and change your stop loss every hour. By doing this, you will be taken out of your position fairly quickly once the intraday trend has reversed itself.

■ *Three-bar stop loss procedure.* In addition to the hourly or half hourly follow-up stop loss procedure recommended above, consider using a trailing stop loss below the lowest low of the last three price bars for long positions and above the highest high of the last three price bars for short positions. In other words, if the last three 5-minute price bars show lows of 34.50, 34.20, and 33.97, then your trailing stop loss for a long position would be below 33.97, since this is the lowest of the three lows. When the next bar posts you can change your stop loss if necessary. In the case of a short position, your trailing stop loss will be above the highest of high the last three price bars.

Remember that these stop losses must be mental stop losses. Don't keep changing your stop loss every 5 minutes, or both you and your broker will go crazy, and you will be reprimanded.

Delayed Gap Open Signals (DGO)

On occasion a market will make a very large gap opening up or down. The gap size (difference between previous day's low or high and the open) will be much larger than usual. In such cases, the market will need to make a considerable move up in the case of a gap lower opening, or down in the case of a gap higher opening, before it can trigger entry on the first gap method (GO) I have just described. By the time this occurs, a great deal of the day's potential profit may have passed you by. In order to deal with this situation, I have developed the *delayed gap open method* (DGO) which is designed to provide entry more quickly, and which may be used in conjunction with the first gap method I discussed, thereby resulting in two possible entry signals on any given day. See Figure 6-5 for the ideal GDO buy signal. Here's how the method works.

Delayed Gap Down Buy Signal

1. *Gap lower opening.* In the event of a gap lower opening, you will place a buy stop two ticks above the low of the previous day. This is similar to the basic GO method.

2. *If at the end of the first hour of trading the buy stop has not been elected,* in other words if the market has not triggered you on the long side, you will examine the current price in relation to the current day's opening price. If the current price is higher than the opening price by two ticks after the end of the first hour of trading, you will enter the long position at market. Let me review this. *If at the end of the first hour of trading*

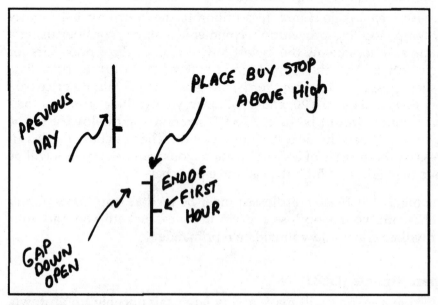

Figure 6-5. Delayed gap down buy signal.

the traditional buy gap stop order has not been hit, you will check the current price and the opening price for the day. If the current price is above the open, you will buy at the market. Your initial stop loss will be either a money management stop loss or a stop loss several ticks below the low of the day at the time you are filled.

3. *If the current price at the end of the first hour is below the opening price,* you will enter a buy stop two ticks above the current high of the day. *Furthermore, you may also retain your original buy stop two ticks above the low of the previous day in the event that the market begins to make a very large move in the anticipated direction. Should this occur, you will then be long multiple units capitalizing hopefully on both possible signals.* See Figure 6-6.

Delayed Gap Up Sell Signal

1. *In the event of a gap higher open,* the initial procedure will be the same as the original gap method (GO). You will enter a sell stop two ticks below the high of the previous day.

2. *After the first hour of trading,* you will check the market. If the current price is below the opening price, you will sell short at the market using either a risk management dollar stop or a stop loss several ticks above the current high of the day.

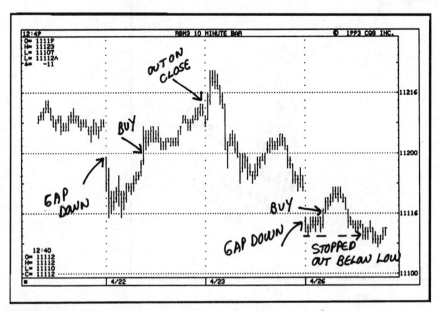

Figure 6-6. Delayed gap down buy signal actual example.

3. *If the market is not below the opening price,* you will enter a sell stop order two ticks below the then-current low of the day in order to get you short. *In addition, you may retain your original gap-sell-stop two ticks below the high of the previous day in the event that the market begins to move strongly down, thereby giving you two units on the short side.*

Figures 6-7 and 6-8 illustrate the 1-hour delay gap sell signal.

As you can see, the one hour gap signal is a technique which allows quicker entry in the event of potentially large moves on the opening, which could limit the potential profit from a delayed buy gap or a delayed sell gap. The best time to use this approach is of course in markets which have opened on significantly large gaps down or up from the previous day's low. Finally, remember, that the DGO requires waiting one hour. I have not experimented with different time delays.

Some Observations about the Gap Technique

I've said previously that the gap technique is one of my favorite day-trading methods. I say this because I have seen many instances in which the gaps have worked extremely well and have produced very signifi-

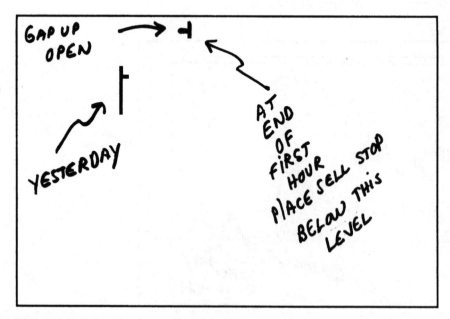

Figure 6-7. Delayed gap up sell signal.

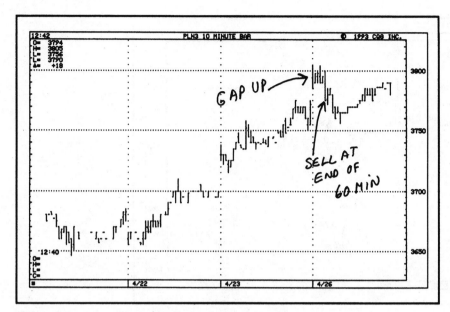

Figure 6-8. Delayed gap up sell signal actual example.

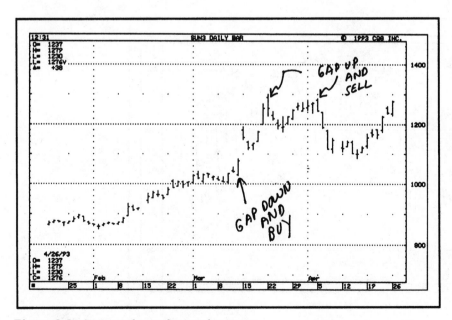

Figure 6-9. Gap signal actual examples, sugar.

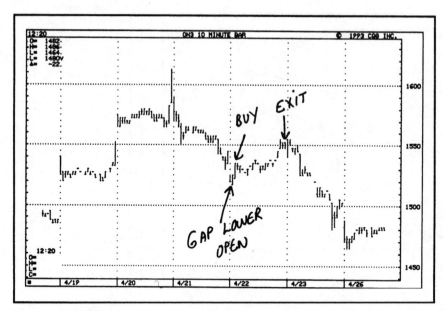

Figure 6-10. Gap signal actual example, oats.

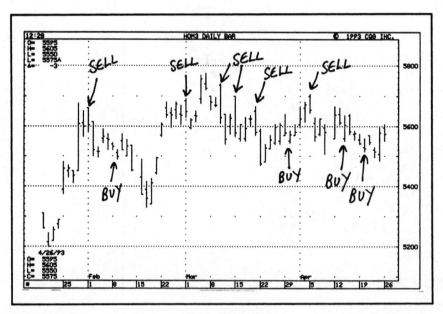

Figure 6-11. Gap signal actual examples, heating oil.

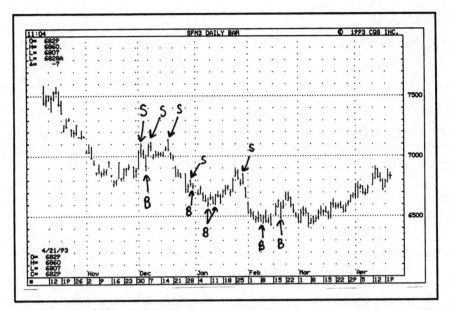

Figure 6-12. Gap signal actual examples, Swiss franc.

cant intraday price moves. Naturally, it is important to remember that *this approach should be used primarily in markets which will have sufficient intraday volatility to permit reasonably profitable moves.* Among my favorites for the gap trades are S&P, currency, treasury bond, crude oil, and precious metals futures. But this list will not be constant; it will change as a function of market conditions and trading volume.

History shows that some of the largest intraday price moves have occurred following gap higher or gap lower openings, particularly following a major news event or government report. One thing I like to look at in terms of gaps is the direction of the market prior to the gap. I've found that if the market has been trending down for a fairly extended period and if the gap lower opening is prompted by bearish news then the signal tends to be more accurate as well as offering greater dollar potential if it occurs. However, a gap higher opening following a bullish trend and bullish news which then turns into a gap sell signal tends to produce very good profits with reasonably low risk. Therefore, I would suggest very strongly that you monitor markets very closely for gap openings following bearish or bullish reports.

Gap trades also seem to work better with market sentiment as a filter. This will be explained more fully later on when I discuss my DSI (daily sentiment index).

Get Some Experience

Although the two techniques I have just described are very simple to understand and implement, they do require some experience. Before using them, I strongly suggest you monitor some markets closely, or get some price charts and mark the gap signals on the price charts so that you will see for yourself how they have developed and how accurate they've been. I reiterate that these two are among my favorite approaches for day trading and I expect they will serve you well, at times triggering major intraday price swings and potentially very large profits.

Remember, however, that *you can't trade a gap unless you trade a gap.* **Unfortunately, too many traders** *fail to enter their gap signals until well after the penetration has occurred, therefore missing many profitable opportunities.*

If you are going to trade gaps, then by all means be organized, watch those markets when they open, find the gaps, and enter your orders. If you don't, then the method won't work for you.

What do gaps mean for the longer term? From the perspective of a day trader, this question is irrelevant. Unfortunately, too many traders think too much. The human mind not only seeks answers to questions but also attempts to extrapolate beyond the current data and beyond the rules hoping that relationships will be found which may allow us to predict the future. To be perfectly honest with you, this is anathema to the day trader.

The day trader must not think beyond today.

The day trader must not attempt to think about what may happen tomorrow as a result of what has happened today.

The gap lower, gap higher opening signals discussed in this chapter have nothing to do with the market's potential moves up or down tomorrow, the next day, or the next day. Therefore, I urge you *not to be tempted to hold a gap position overnight no matter how well it has worked for you during the day. The day trader seeks to establish a day relationship and once the day is over the relationship is over as well.*

Gap Size and Penetration Size

As you know, some price gaps are relatively small while others are relatively large. In researching the gap trades I've found that larger price gaps tend to produce more reliable (i.e., more accurate) signals. I've also found that just a one-tick penetration is less reliable than a two- or five-tick penetration. The ideal gap size and penetration size for each market is slightly different and will vary over time depending on market volatility and price level. I suggest you monitor your results carefully as to gap size and penetration size.

What You Can Realistically Expect

There are system developers and promoters who will lead you astray, promising you riches untold if you follow their trading systems. The fact of the matter is, that *very few, if any, systems can be applied to the market totally mechanically* for the purpose of generating vast profits. The fact is that day trading, whether by the gap method or any other method, is a business and a skill. It must be learned from the ground up. The parameters and rules I've given you are valuable and I believe effective, but you are the individual who must implement them in order to generate the profits. And this, my friends, is not an easy proposition.

As you well know, there are myriad factors which impede the path to profitable day trading, whether you are using gaps or any of the other methods described in this book. Therefore, what you can realistically expect is that *at first you will find the gaps effective, had you done what the gaps told you to do. Unfortunately, there will be many cases in which you will say to yourself "I should have, I would have, or I could have."* These are all excuses. You must follow the gap trades religiously using a certain amount of artistic judgment. However, this is not always easy. One thing I can assure you, however, is that the more you do it, the easier it becomes. And that is certainly helpful.

Realistically, you can expect to make several hundred dollars per contract on average in the gap trades in active markets with a high tick value (i.e., S&P, T-bonds) once you have mastered the techniques. This would be a minimum expectation. The rest would depend on your skill as a trader, your willingness to assume more risk by trading larger positions, and your skill in entering and exiting multiple contracts using some of the techniques I have discussed in this chapter.

In closing, I reiterate that many extremely large moves have occurred following gap higher or gap lower openings. Pay close attention to the markets, follow those gaps, and when the big moves occur, you will be on board. If you're not following the gap signals closely, then you can't be on board the big moves. It's that simple. While this may sound ridiculous to you, the fact is, that *many day traders miss big moves by not following their timing indicators or systems.* If you're going to be a follower of the gap trades, and if you have studied them sufficiently to have confidence in their potential, then by all means trade them religiously.

A Few Last Words about Stop Orders

Some of you may be adverse to using buy stops or sell stops as the entry method for the gap trade or for the purpose of risk management. Although you may be suspicious of having resting orders in the markets, thinking perhaps that they will get you or that the floor will run the stops, you are wrong. This may happen on occasion, but I sincerely feel it is the exception rather than the rule. In very thinly traded markets you may not wish to use such orders; however, in the more active orders I see no problem with using stop orders. If, however, you are still overcome with suspicion and paranoia about the trading floor, then I strongly suggest that you use either a stop limit order or that you not place an order at all, taking the chance that the market will run right through your price without your being filled.

Consider using stop limit orders where the exchange accepts them. They can be very effective. *As you know, however, there will be instances in which stop limit orders will not be filled; therefore, you will have no position when in fact you should have.* In the vast majority of cases, stop limit orders will work in your favor. Should you find, however, that your stop limit order was not filled due to fast market conditions, then leave the order active. In many cases the market will come back to your price and you will be filled. The risk of using stop limit orders is that you will not be filled. It's a chance you have to take if resting stop orders concern you.

7

Support and Resistance: the MAC

Perhaps two of the oldest, most well known, and most time-tested ideas in stock and futures trading are support and resistance. As the names imply, support and resistance are specific price areas or price levels which either support prices on declines in up trends or which resist prices on rallies in down trends. In an up trend, short-term and day traders will attempt to buy at support or at levels of support. In a down trend, short-term and day traders will attempt to sell at resistance levels or in resistance areas.

The concept makes a great deal of sense. No matter how complex or intricate methods of market analysis and trading systems become through the years, ideas of support and resistance have been pervasive and enduring. The only problem with these ideas is that they require a reasonably objective method for determining support and resistance in order that trades may be entered based on these ideas. If support and resistance cannot be determined, then you cannot define concise levels or areas in which to establish and/or exit positions. Therefore, it behooves traders as well as investors to develop effective strategies and technical methodologies for calculating or determining support and resistance levels.

For many years such levels have been determined using a wide range of tools such as support and resistance trend lines, various chart formations, Gann angles, ratio retracements, Fibonnaci numbers, the golden mean constant, point and figure charts, and others too numerous to mention. Many arcane methods have been employed in efforts to determine support and resistance, some successful at times, others successful frequently, and all too many unsuccessful a vast majority of the time.

Regardless of the fads in market timing methods which have occurred in the futures markets since the 1950s, ideas of support and resistance have endured, and with good reason. *The simple fact of the matter is, that if calculated correctly, they work.* It is the purpose of this chapter to explain and illustrate for you my ideas of support and resistance, in particular as they pertain to the day trader.

The day trader is in an advantageous position when it comes to the use of support and resistance levels, inasmuch as the day trader's relationship with the market ends when the day is over. Therefore, a bad decision or a bad position which was entered based on expectations of support or resistance *will not return the next day to haunt the trader.* As I have said many times in this book, *the single greatest benefit of day trading is to force exit of positions by the end of the day.* A day trader who does not do so is not a day trader and will, of course, suffer the consequences of riding positions beyond their ideal exit.

Determining support and resistance levels is somewhat different for the day trader than it is for the position trader. This is because *support and resistance levels for the day trader must be closer to the current market price than they are for the long-term or position trader.* Markets can only drop so far in one day (in most cases), and consequently the determination of support and resistance levels by the day trader must be realistic in terms of what can be expected. This does not mean that the day trader must "chase the markets." It does, however, mean that day traders *must be willing to use realistic technical support and resistance levels in order to establish their positions.*

As I mentioned earlier, there have been many attempts through the years to develop methods which will define support and resistance levels as precisely as possible. I wouldn't be surprised if there are as many traders as there are techniques. However, I have developed a technique which has shown itself to be extremely valuable and highly specific. Although this technique was originally developed for use in long-term trading, I have found it to be applicable to short-term and day trading.

The Moving Average Channel

Borrowing from concepts originally introduced in the 1950s by Richard Donchian, I departed from the traditional use of moving averages. I conducted intensive research on moving average channels (MACs) which consisted of a moving average of high prices and a moving average of low prices. Rather than focus on closing prices, I felt that support and resistance should be determined using high and low prices, since high and low prices are specifically geared to ideas of support and resistance.

Typically, resistance tends to be found near previous highs, and support tends to be found near previous lows. It therefore occurred to me that rather than examine moving averages of closing prices for support or resistance, it might be better to use moving averages of lows and highs to determine support and resistance respectively. What I discovered took me several years to fully believe and several more to implement.

My technique uses a moving average of the high and a moving average of the low in conjunction which form a moving average channel that is used for determining support and resistance. Figure 7-1 illustrates the MAC used on a 5-minute chart. As you can see, the channel has some distinct characteristics:

1. *When the trend of prices is up, the MAC tends to act as support.* In other words, as price declines to the lower portion of the channel, the moving average of lows (MAL) tends to find support.

2. *When the trend of prices is down, the MAC tends to act as resistance.* In bear trends, rallies to the top of the channel, the moving average of highs (MAH) tends to serve as resistance.

3. *When price bars are completely outside the top of the channel, the price trend is strongly bullish.* Please refer to Figure 7-1.

4. *When price bars are completely below the bottom of the channel, the price trend is very bearish.* See Figure 7-1.

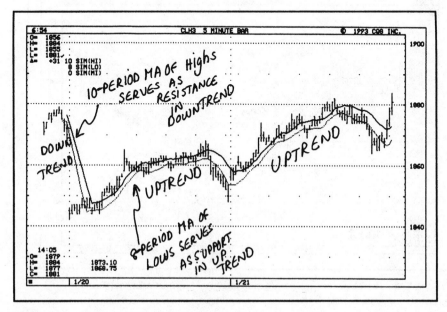

Figure 7-1. Characteristics of the MAC.

Figures 7-2 and 7-3 further illustrate the relationship between the MAC high and low and prices. Please note that I have indicated support and resistance levels accordingly. Can you think of how these levels might be used?

How Support and Resistance Develop during the Day

Please examine Figure 7-4. It consists of several frames which illustrate how support and resistance patterns develop during the day in relation to the MAC. As you can see, prices tend to bounce off their support levels. The purpose of the channel is to define precise areas of support and resistance. *In an up trend, the day trader will attempt to buy when price enters a support area and sell when price enters a resistance area in a down-trending market.* The key is to specifically define the following:

1. The trend
2. Support and resistance

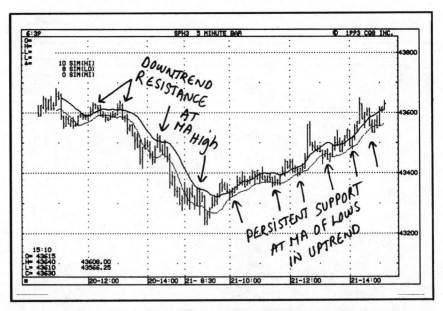

Figure 7-2. The MAC on an S&P intraday chart—support and resistance.

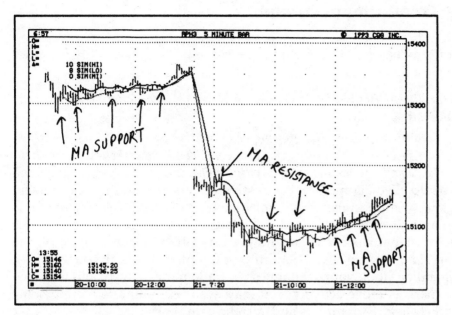

Figure 7-3. The MAC on an intraday British pound chart—support and resistance.

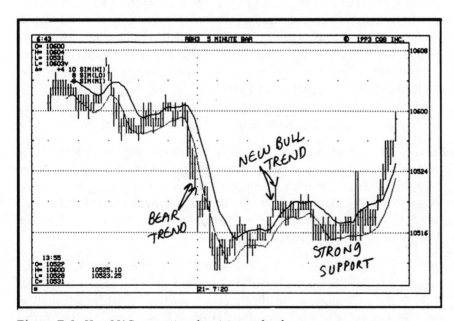

Figure 7-4. How MAC support and resistance develop.

Determining Trend, Support, and Resistance

In order to use the MAC technique for day trading, the following rules will be used:

- *Determine if the market is in an up trend or in a down trend.* This is achieved as follows.

- *If, at any time after market opening or on market opening, the market develops two successive 5-minute price bars completely above the top of the channel (i.e., above the moving average of the high),* then the trend is presumed to be up. (See Figure 7-4). Aggressive traders who wish to circumvent buying at support may buy immediately upon the development of this signal; however, this procedure entails considerably more risk. Once such a signal has occurred, the predisposition or bias will be on the long side. You can use 10-minute or 20-minute bars if you wish, or, depending upon your willingness to trade more actively and to watch the markets move actively, you may even use 3-minute bars in some markets (e.g., S&P futures and currencies at times).

- *Presuming a bullish bias, the day trader will determine the specific price level of the MAL.* This specific price level will also be called the *lower buy point* (LBP). Conservative day traders will enter orders to buy at the LBP or will be watching the market for declines to the LBP in order to buy at the market once this has occurred. Figure 7-5 illustrates this procedure. The moving average of highs (MAH) is also called the *higher buy point* (HBP). Aggressive traders will buy as prices return to "test" the HBP. In practice, however, the HBP is often too high a level at which to buy. Most traders are better off calculating the midpoint of the MAC by adding the MAL and the MAH and dividing by 2. This yields the midpoint of the channel or the (MBP) *mid buy point.*

As the day progresses you will want to maintain resting orders at the MBP or, if you're a very conservative day trader, at the LBP. If you have a quote system that will track these points for you, triggering an audible alarm when these levels are hit, you can place orders accordingly. This is a procedure which requires time and effort; however, it can yield substantial rewards if properly carried out.

- *Presuming a bearish bias, the day trader will determine the specific price level of the MAH.* This specific price level will also be called the *upper sell point* (USP). Conservative day traders will enter orders to sell at the USP or will be watching the market for rallies to the USP in order to sell at the market once this has occurred. Figure 7-6 illustrates this procedure. MAH is also called the *lower sell point* (LSP). Aggressive

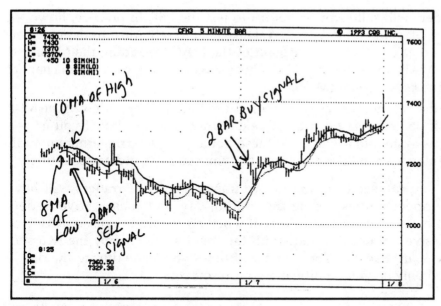

Figure 7-5. The MAC points defined, coffee futures.

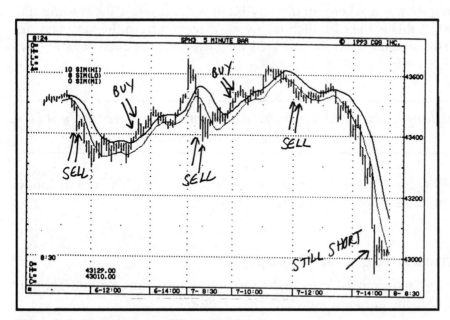

Figure 7-6. The MAC points defined, S&P futures.

traders will sell as prices return to test the LSP. In practice, however, the USP is often too low a level at which to sell. Most traders are better off calculating the midpoint of the MAC by adding the MAL and the MAH and dividing by 2. This yields the midpoint of the channel or the *mid sell point* (MSP).

■ As the day progresses you will want to have resting orders at the MSP or, if you're a very conservative day trader, at the USP. If you have a quote system that will track these points for you, triggering an audible alarm when these levels are hit, you can place orders accordingly.

As you can see from the illustrations, aggressive traders will have many opportunities during the trading day, and conservative traders won't have as many. Regardless of whether you trade conservatively or aggressively, you must trade with the trend as defined by the two-successive-bar breakout. The number of times you trade during the day is limited only by your ability and your resources.

Trading within an Established Trend

Frequently the market will already be in a trend when the trading day begins. If this is the case then take your direction from the very last signal. This signal may have occurred the day before or even several days ago. Remember that

> *The longer the trend has been in existence, the more likely it is to reverse itself, so be cautious.*

See Figure 7-7. Naturally, if the trend reverses itself you will follow the indicated procedures for the given trend.

Exiting Positions, Right or Wrong

Well, I've told you how and when to get in, now how do you get out? The following are some suggested exit methods.

Stop Loss.   The procedure here is simple enough. You have two choices. Either set a predetermined dollar risk stop loss, which will vary from market to market, or exit on technical action.

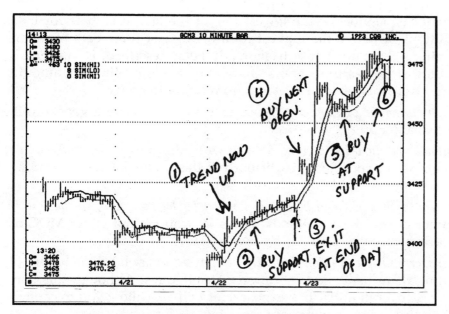

Figure 7-7. Using the MAC to trade within an established trend.

If you enter a long position on a decline to the LBP, then you can exit if there are two consecutive bars outside the MAL, which would, of course, constitute a sell signal. If you enter a long on the UBP, then you can use the same exit procedure, knowing, of course, that it entails more dollar risk since you entered at a higher price. A happy medium is buying at the MBP, the middle of the channel. I prefer to use technical action in the form of a reversing signal to exit my trades as opposed to the use of a dollar risk stop loss for this technique.

If you enter a short position on a rally to the USP, then you can exit if there are two consecutive bars outside the MAH, which would, of course, constitute a buy signal. If you enter a short on the LSP, then you can use the same exit procedure, knowing, of course, that it entails more dollar risk since you entered at a lower price. A happy medium is selling at the MSP, the middle of the channel. I prefer to use technical action in the form of a reversing signal to exit my trades as opposed to the use of a dollar risk stop loss for this technique.

Trailing Stop Loss. Trailing stop losses should be used once a position has started to move strongly in your favor. I have a number of suggestions to offer you in this respect, all based on extensive personal experience.

- *Trail a stop loss* below the lowest low of the last three bars for long positions or above the highest high or the last three bars for short positions. This procedure has already been described. Do not use a trailing stop loss until you show a reasonable profit. This amount varies from market to market and from trader to trader.

- *Use a stochastic exit signal* as your exit once you have a good profit. (See Chapter 5.)

- *Exit at a specific price target* and do so when the market has "bulged" or "cratered" in your favor, particularly if this occurs late in the trading session.

- *Remember that you will be out of your trades by the end of the day,* so if neither of the above methods works for you get out either MOC or shortly before the close.

- *Consider multiple positions on entry* so that you may have the luxury of exiting them using several different techniques. Although this may increase overall initial risk exposure, it will also allow you to capitalize on strong trends which are consistent with your position.

Sideways Trend Trading—Trading within the Channel

Another good procedure for using the MAC as a day-trading vehicle is to trade within the channel. This simply means that in an up trend, you will attempt to buy retracements to the moving average of the lows and exit these positions when prices have rallied to the moving average of the highs or higher. Then, when prices decline once again to the moving average of the lows (if they do), you will buy again hoping to sell on a rally to the moving average of the highs or higher. For those traders who would like to maintain their positions once they are established at the MAL, a stop loss under the MAL by several ticks may be used. Therefore, the position may be carried through to the end of the day in order to take advantage of the trend should it continue.

When selling at the MAH in a down trend, the trader will attempt to take profits once prices decline to the MAL, hoping to reestablish short positions on a rally to the MAH. Both of these procedures, however, tend to limit profits, since you are cutting profits short not knowing whether the trend will continue in your favor.

The best time to use the above techniques is when there is no defined trend. In other words, when the market is moving relatively sideways within the MAC, this technique can allow you to trade many times, buying MAL support and selling MAH resistance. As an example, consider Figure 7-8, which illustrates my point.

A Few Precautions and Suggestions

Because the MAC technique I have just described is a trading method and not a system, you must be aware that it is adjustable to the needs of the trader and will not work in the same fashion for all traders who use it. Once you begin to use this technique, you will develop individual adaptation to the methodology which may suit your purposes better than what has been described herein.

This technique may not, in fact, be suitable for all traders. You must find your own place with it, and you must determine whether this is the technique you wish to use. For those who are interested in trading frequently for small moves within the day and within an established trend, I believe that this technique is ideal. If the trend should change drastically during the day you will be stopped out of your position, and you will then, provided there is sufficient time left during the day, have the opportunity to trade from the other side of the market.

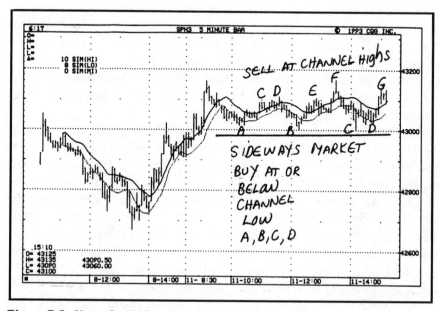

Figure 7-8. Using the MAC to day trade a trendless market.

In many respects, using the MAC technique for day trading is similar to riding a bicycle. A book can only go so far in explaining to you how the job is done. Thereafter you must take the initiative, you must have the discipline, and you must take the risk in order to make the technique work for you. What I have provided in this chapter, although I have tried to be as specific as possible, is merely the framework of a technique which combines science and skill. If you are a serious day trader who is looking for numerous opportunities to buy up support and sell at resistance, I know of few techniques which can provide the many opportunities that this one can. Yes, there will be days and there will be times when this technique does not afford you an opportunity, and there will be losing days. However, if you are consistent with it, you will find that there are many opportunities within trends to establish positions using the channel and to exit these positions profitably.

Because the channel technique is not totally mechanical and involves some degree of subjectivity, I urge you to work with it before implementing it so that you may adapt it to your particular needs and your particular style of trading to this method.

Using the Channel Technique with Other Methods

The MAC technique is especially easy to use in conjunction with some of the other day-trading methods I've discussed in this book. Specifically, the channel technique works extremely well once another trading system or method has triggered an entry on the long or short side. Say, for example, that either of the two gap-trading techniques triggers a buy. In this case you would use the MAC as a method of buying on reactions to the longer support level of the channel.

Assume that S&P futures give a gap buy signal early in the day. Assume also that the buy signal entry price is 399.50. Typically, the first response of the market would be to push through 399.50 rather quickly, possibly moving to as high as 400+. Thereafter, the market would typically (but not always) retrace its gains perhaps moving back down to 399.60 or lower. It may be that 399.60 is the bottom of the MAC and, therefore, a place to go long following the initial burst of activity to the up side.

I have provided three concise illustrations of this situation in Figures 7-9, 7-10, and 7-11. Examine them carefully and note my comments. As you can see, the MAC is a very versatile technique which easily lends itself to use with other day-trading systems and methods. No matter how you decide to use the MAC, remember that within the rules I've given you this is strictly a day-trading method.

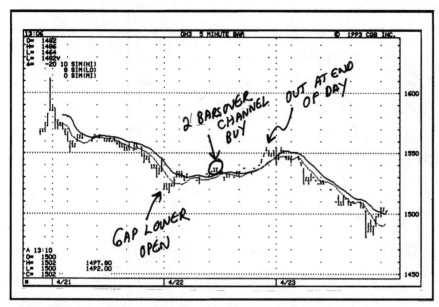

Figure 7-9. Using the MAC for entry following a gap buy signal.

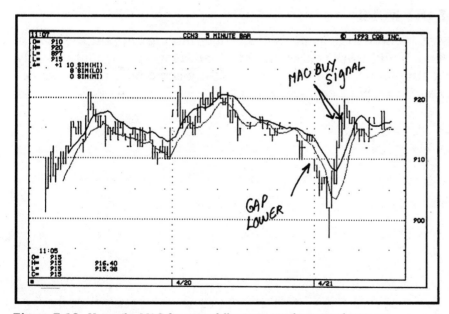

Figure 7-10. Using the MAC for entry following a gap buy signal in cocoa.

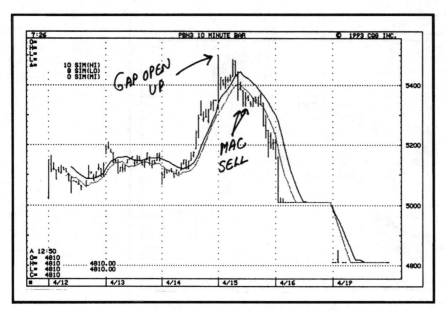

Figure 7-11. Using the MAC for entry following a gap sell signal in pork bellies.

Evaluation of the MAC

The MAC is an excellent method for determining support, resistance, and trend. It will work well on intraday data as well as on daily, weekly, and monthly data. It does, however, require some judgment inasmuch as it is not a totally mechanical method.

8

Using Wilder's RSI
for Day Trading

The *relative strength index (RSI)* was originally developed by Welles
Wilder. In the early 1980s when I was on a seminar tour of the Far East
with Welles and a group of other traders, he was just beginning to
develop his applications for the RSI. Since then there have been many
applications of the RSI, all of which have potential, but many of which
will not generate profits for the day trader.

The RSI is a price-based oscillator. It has many applications both as an
index of overbought/oversold market conditions and as a timing indicator. Of particular importance to day traders is the first derivative RSI
which tends to smooth the indicator, thereby resulting in fewer false signals and greater accuracy in day trading.

Before discussing the first derivative of RSI as a day-trading indicator,
I will explain the raw RSI indicator as traditionally used by futures
traders. This understanding is necessary in order for you to differentiate
between my suggested applications and the application commonly used
by contemporary futures traders.

In many respects, the RSI is similar to stochastics in that it is used as
an oscillator. Subsequent to extremely high readings, a sell signal is indicated when RSI begins to decline. Conversely, a low RSI that begins to
increase in value while prices are low is a buy signal. There are many
different applications of RSI.

Since the RSI lends itself equally to many different interpretations, I
won't claim here that my suggested methodology regarding the use of
RSI is unique. I do feel, however, that my first derivative application is a
unique implementation of RSI. Figure 8-1 shows RSI application along
with my comments.

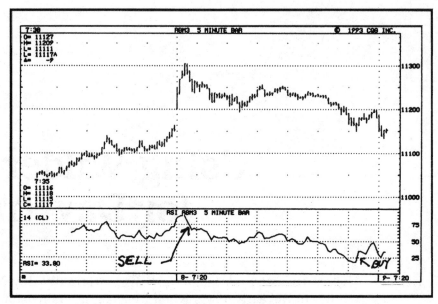

Figure 8-1. Traditional use of relative strength index (RSI).

Defining the First Derivative

Don't let the term *first derivative* scare you into thinking that complicated mathematics is involved. In fact, it is not. The first derivative of any variable is defined as

---

A quantity derived through the mathematical manipulation of a previous quantity.

In other words, as this relates to the futures markets, consider the following: If I calculate the RSI in a given market, and if I then use the RSI as the raw value for calculating a moving average of the RSI, then the second calculation, namely the moving average of the RSI, is the first derivative of the RSI. If I calculate an RSI of the moving average of RSI, then I have calculated a third derivative of the RSI. Figure 8-2 shows an RSI plotted against its first derivative.

My work with timing indicators as well as derivatives of timing indicators has convinced me that such manipulation of the data can be very effective in terms of generating meaningful and less random timing signals. Although there is insufficient space here to launch into a discus-

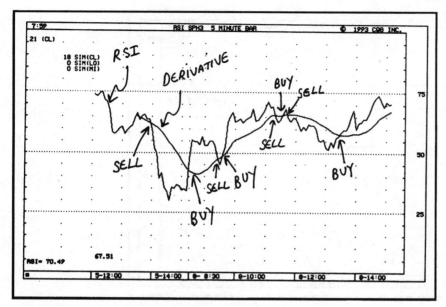

Figure 8-2. RSI and its first derivative.

sion of indicator derivatives and their comparisons, I would urge you to undertake such studies on your own. You may be impressed, as I have been, with the results.

A first, second, third, and fourth derivative, and so on, then, are quantities derived from previous indicators which are themselves derivatives of other indicators or raw prices.

Let me give you a concrete example of what I mean by a first derivative of the RSI. Figure 8-3 shows an intraday market with a 14-day RSI indicator plotted against price. Figure 8-4 now shows the same indicator plotted against price, however, also included is the first derivative of RSI. As you can see, the derivative line is smoother, less choppy, and therefore, in my opinion, more readily usable by futures traders. Figures 8-5 and 8-6 show two different derivatives of RSI plotted against the same price chart. Examine these if you will, and reach your own conclusion, strictly based on visual observation, as to which of the three might have potential as a timing indicator.

Rules for Day Trading with the RSI

Here are some rules for using the RSI and its first derivative for day trading.

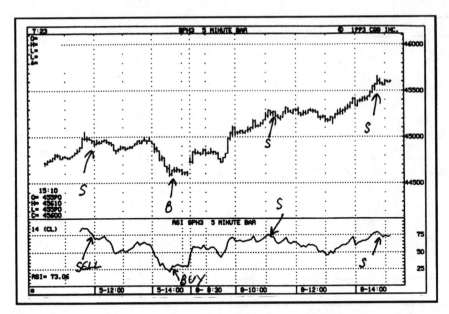

Figure 8-3. Intraday market with a 14-day RSI indicator plotted against price.

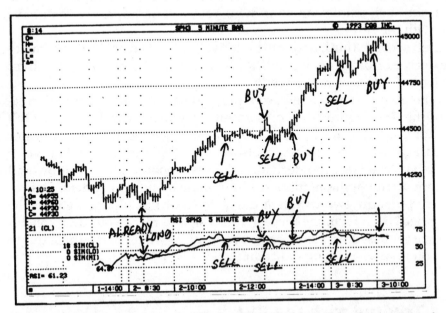

Figure 8-4. Intraday market with a 14-day RSI indicator plotted against price and the first derivative of RSI.

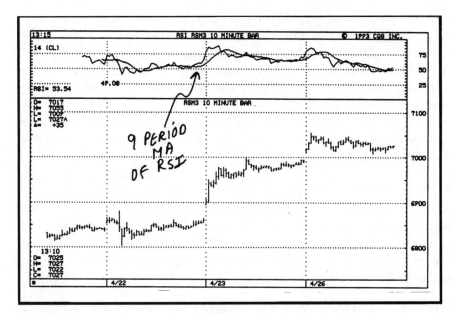

Figure 8-5. A derivative of RSI plotted against price, 9-period MA.

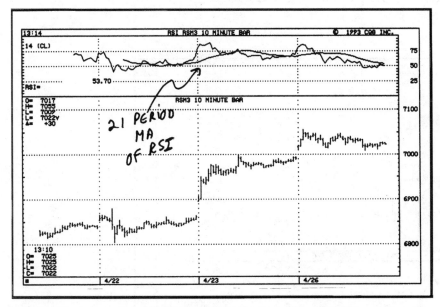

Figure 8-6. A derivative of RSI plotted against price, 21-period MA.

1. Using RSI as an overbought or oversold timing indicator is very simple. Select your cutoff points (as you do with stochastics). If, for example, you select 25 and 75, then your procedures would be as follows:

    a. When RSI drops to 25 or lower and then turns back above 25 you buy and use a stop loss either under the lowest most recent low or a risk management stop loss.

    b. When RSI has been at 75 or higher then sell short when it declines below 75 using a stop loss above the most recent high or use a dollar risk management stop loss.

    For procedures *a* and *b* you can vary the values. Figure 8-7 shows the use of a 9-period RSI on 30-minute S&P data with 15 and 85 as the cutoff points. Note my buy and sell points on the chart. As you can see, RSI is a valuable tool for the day trader. Note that RSI turned bullish on 12/9 and remained so through 12/19. This gave the day trader an opportunity to buy every day so long as the bias was bullish because of the bullish RSI.

2. Using the first derivative of RSI (or other derivatives if you wish) is like using an oscillator. The procedure is simple:

    a. When RSI falls below its first derivative, sell short and either use a stop loss as the reversal signal (i.e., RSI closing above its derivative) or use a dollar risk stop loss.

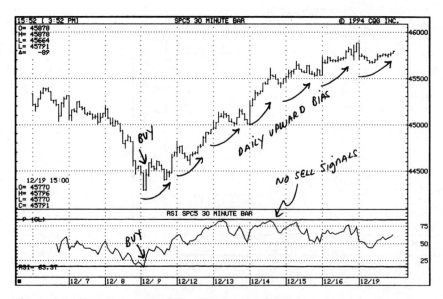

Figure 8-7. Using a 9-period RSI on 30-minute S&P data.

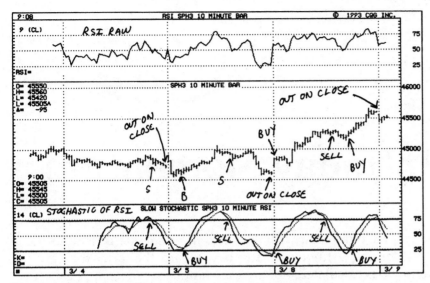

Figure 8-8. A stochastic first derivative of RSI versus price.

b. When RSI goes above its first derivative, then buy with a stop loss either as a signal reversal or as a dollar risk stop.

In all cases you must remember that a signal is *not activated until the time segment has ended.* In other words, if you are using a 5-minute chart, RSI will change every time the market has changed price; *it is only the RSI value at the end of the 5-minute segment that's considered for timing signal purposes.*

A Suggestion

Before leaving the RSI, I'll share with you an idea which I've just started to research which I feel has incredible potential. If you use a 14-period slow stochastic as your first derivative of RSI, you'll find that your signals will be even more accurate. What do I mean? I mean that instead of calculating the stochastic on price, you will calculate a stochastic of RSI. This can be easily done on the CQG (Commodity Quote Graphics) system as well as on others. Examine Figure 8-8 along with my comments on the chart. I feel strongly that this approach has outstanding potential for day trading and that it should be pursued aggressively. There are many other possibilities. Consider using an RSI of the RSI as a derivative, or for that matter another indicator applied to the RSI that will act as a smoothing factor. The idea here is, of course, to reduce the number of false or losing signals by making RSI less sensitive but at the same time not delaying its response to changing market conditions.

9

Using Intraday Momentum

Many traders are unfamiliar with the *momentum indicator* or with its value as an aid in timing. Although many have heard the term, they are not aware of how it is calculated, nor are they familiar with its applications.

Momentum is a very simple indicator which is easily calculated. In order to calculate the 1-day momentum (MOM), simply subtract today's price from yesterday's price. The result is a 1-day MOM. Therefore, if today's price is $52 and yesterday's price is $53, then the 1-day momentum would be −1. If today's price is $52 and yesterday's price was $50, then today's 1-day momentum would be +2.

As you can see, the calculation of a 1-day momentum index is extremely simple. To calculate a 2-day momentum index, subtract the price 2 days ago from today's price. For calculating 3-, 4-, 5-day momentum, follow the same procedure.

Momentum is a rate change indicator, since it provides you with an idea of trend strength. When momentum is moving down very quickly, it is an indication that prices are changing rapidly on the down side with large price moves. When momentum is rising rapidly, it is an indication that the market is trending strongly higher. Momentum can be used as a trading indicator by applying some simple rules.

This chapter will illustrate some suggested applications of intraday momentum for the purpose of day trading. I will show you some very interesting applications of momentum; however, I stress at the outset that these are merely applications and *not systems*. They are trading techniques which you will need to work with and refine. I believe that they have considerable potential, but they will require work.

Figure 9-1 shows an intraday price chart versus a 21-day momentum indicator. As you can see, MOM is like an oscillator. It fluctuates above and below a zero line. When MOM crosses from negative to positive, an uptrend is likely, and when it crosses from positive to negative a decline is likely.

As with most oscillators, MOM is good at finding trends; however, it gives many false signals as it "flutters" above and below zero. Regardless of this limitation, MOM can be used very effectively for position and day trading by comparing it to its first derivative. This is a simple procedure. All we need to do is to plot MOM against a moving average of itself (which is its first derivative).

Figure 9-2 shows the same market as Figure 9-1 but with an 18-period MA of the 21-period MOM. As you can see, by buying and selling when MOM crosses above and below its MA line, many of the false start signals are eliminated.

In addition to the use of a moving average of MOM to determine its first derivative, you can use other indicators such as RSI, stochastics, or rate of change (to be discussed in Chapter 10). Figures 9-3 through 9-7 illustrate some of the derivative methods and their signals as used in day trading. The methods and applications discussed in this chapter hold great promise as timing indicators and trading systems; however, considerably more research must be completed before firm conclusions can be reached.

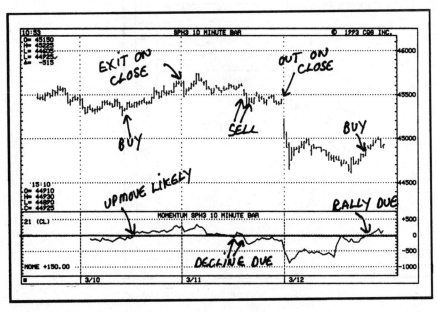

Figure 9-1. 21-period momentum on 10-minute S&P chart.

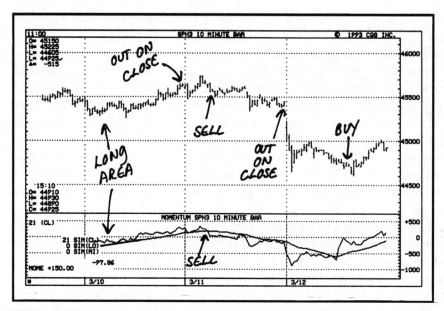

Figure 9-2. 21-period momentum versus 18-period MA of momentum of 10-minute S&P.

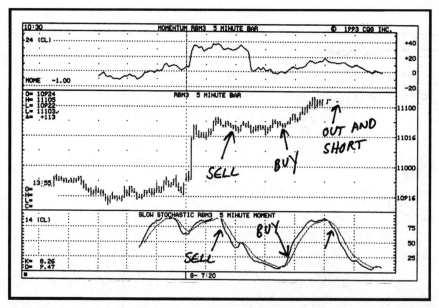

Figure 9-3. The stochastic derivative of momentum—timing signals in 5-minute T-bonds.

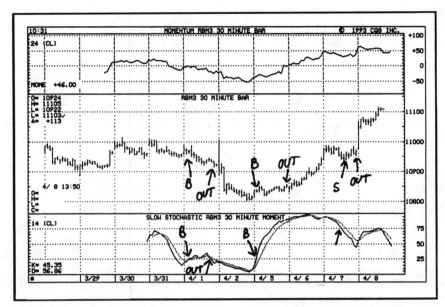

Figure 9-4. The stochastic derivative of momentum—timing signals in 30-minute T-bonds.

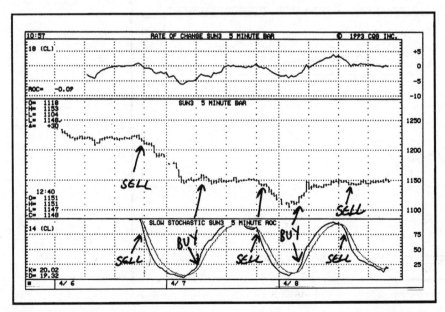

Figure 9-5. The stochastic derivative of momentum—timing signals in 5-minute sugar.

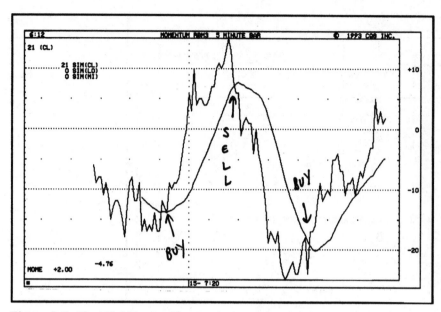

Figure 9-6. The MA derivative of momentum—timing signals, ideal signals.

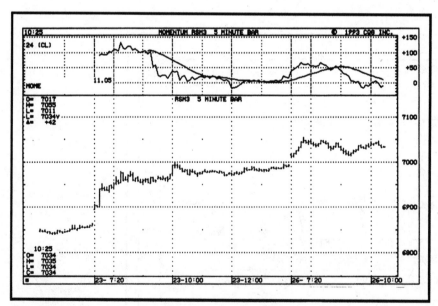

Figure 9-7. The MA derivative of momentum—timing signals in 5-minute Swiss francs.

As you can see, there are several potentially effective derivatives of the momentum indicator which may be used to decrease the number of false signals. The research on these combinations is still very sparse, and I encourage those interested in refining their day-trading techniques to investigate these combinations more thoroughly.

10
Rate of Change in Day Trading

The last chapter discussed momentum as a day trader indicator. This chapter will explain how to use rate of change (ROC) as an intraday timing indicator. While momentum is calculated by subtracting 1 day's price from another, rate of change is determined by dividing 1 day's price by another. Therefore, if yesterday's price was $4 and today's price is $2, we would divide $4 by $2 and arrive at a rate of change of $2. In this case, the momentum as well as the rate of change indicator would have a value of two. If yesterday's price was $7 and today's price was $2, then the rate of change for today would be 3.5, or 7 divided by 2. In this case, the momentum, however, would be 5 (2 subtracted from 7). To calculate a 5-day rate of change, simply divide today's price by the price 5 days ago. It's really that simple.

Figure 10-1 illustrates an intraday price chart plotted against a 1-day ROC, a 3-period ROC, and a 14-period ROC. As you can readily see, the length of the ROC you've selected can make a very big difference in the trades you find.

ROC is essentially an oscillator which is sensitive to changes in market movement which allow us to know ahead of time when a change in price trend is likely to occur. However, ROC cannot tell us whether this change will be a large one or a small one. It can only tell us that the trend is likely to change. Knowing that a change in trend is likely, we can, as day traders, take the necessary action to either limit losses or to enter potentially profitable day trades. ROC as well as MOM both apply to position trades as well.

As you can see, the calculation of a one ROC index is extremely simple. To calculate a two ROC, divide the price 2 days ago from today's price.

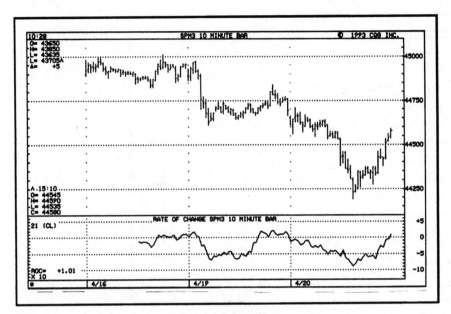

Figure 10-1. 21-period ROC on 10-minute S&P chart.

For calculating 3-, 4-, or 5-day ROC, follow the same procedure. ROC is a rate change indicator, since it provides you with an idea of trend strength. When ROC is moving down very quickly, it is an indication that prices are changing rapidly on the down side with large price moves. When ROC is rising rapidly, it is an indication that the market is trending strongly higher. ROC can be used as a trading indicator by applying some simple rules. This chapter will illustrate some suggested applications of intraday ROC for the purpose of day trading.

Figure 10-1 shows an intraday price chart versus a 21-day ROC indicator. As you can see, ROC is an oscillator. It fluctuates above and below a zero line. When ROC crosses from negative to positive, an uptrend is likely, and when it crosses from positive to negative, a decline is likely. As with most oscillators, ROC is good at finding trends; however, it gives many false signals as it flutters above and below zero.

Regardless of this limitation, ROC can be used very effectively for position and day trading by comparing it to its first derivative. This is a simple procedure. All we need to do is to plot ROC against a moving average of itself (which is its first derivative).

Figure 10-2 shows the same market as Figure 10-1 but with an 18-period MA of the 21-period ROC. As you can see, by buying and selling when ROC crosses above and below its MA line, many of the false start signals are eliminated.

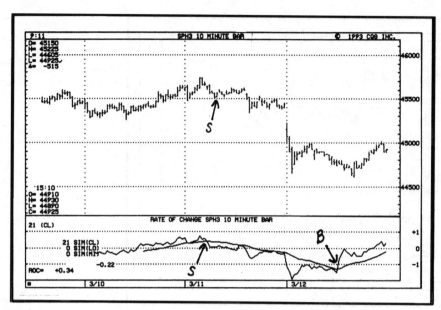

Figure 10-2. 21-period ROC versus 18-period MA of ROC of 10-minute S&P.

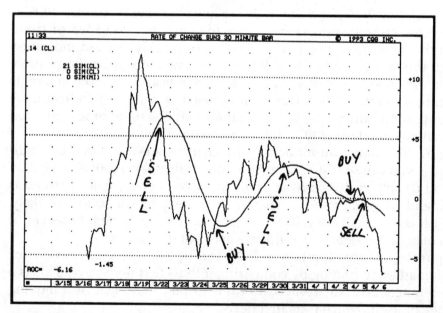

Figure 10-3. The MA derivative of ROC—ideal timing signals.

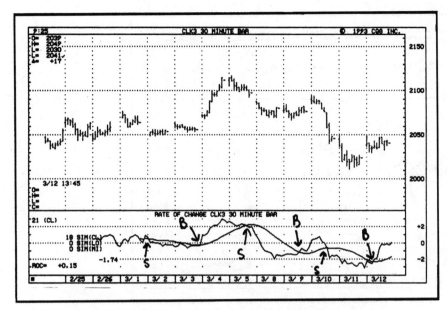

Figure 10-4. The MA derivative of ROC—actual signals, 30-minute crude oil.

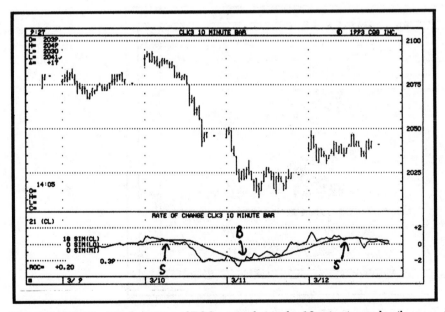

Figure 10-5. The MA derivative of ROC—actual signals, 10-minute crude oil.

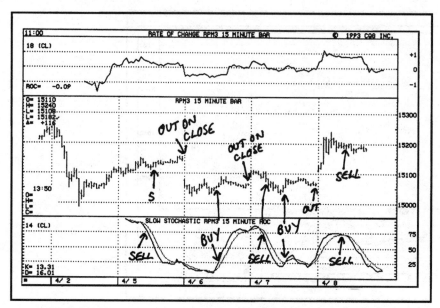

Figure 10-6. The stochastic derivative of ROC—timing signals, British pound.

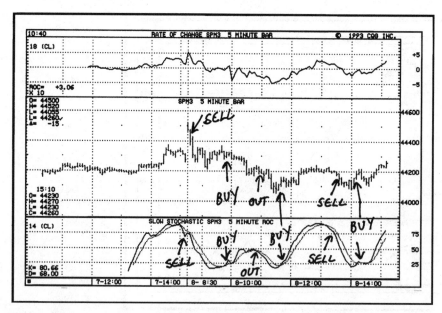

Figure 10-7. The stochastic derivative of ROC—timing signals, S&P.

In addition to the use of a moving average of ROC to determine its first derivative, you can use other indicators such as RSI, stochastics, or momentum (discussed in Chapter 9). Figures 10-3 through 10-7 illustrate some of the different derivative methods and their signals as used in day trading. The methods and applications discussed in this chapter hold great promise as timing indicators and trading systems; however, considerably more research must be completed before firm conclusions can be reached.

As you can see, several potentially effective derivatives of the ROC indicator may be used to decrease the number of false signals. The research on these combinations is still very sparse, and I encourage those who are interested in refining their day-trading techniques to investigate these combinations more thoroughly.

11
Intraday
Channel Breakout

One of the successful techniques used by day traders is based on breaking out on a price break out above resistance or below support. The expectation here is that once a market penetrates above a previous resistance level, the probability is high that the new trend will continue, at least long enough for traders to generate profit. It is also believed, conversely, that if prices fall below a previously established support level, then the market will continue in the down direction sufficiently long to permit short-term traders to take profits. The channel break system for day trading is designed to achieve these goals. If you reflect upon the many occasions in which markets have penetrated their intraday high and then continued higher for the rest of the day, you will recognize the indicator quickly. Similarly, if you consider the many times you've seen prices fall below the day's low only to continue persistently lower for the balance of the day, you will realize the value of this indicator for the purpose of selling short.

Figures 11-1 and 11-2 illustrate the intraday charts showing breakouts above support and below resistance. The channel break system for day trading is designed to capitalize on such breakouts. In other words, the day trader using this approach will be buying on strength and selling on weakness, which is not such a bad idea if you consider the importance of going with the existing trend. Naturally, the other side of the coin here is that those who buy breakouts on the up side or sell breakouts on the down side may be entering positions near at the top of the market or at the bottom of the market as the trend changes, and that risk may therefore lead to losses more frequently than would buying at support or selling at resistance. I will allow the facts in this case, however, to

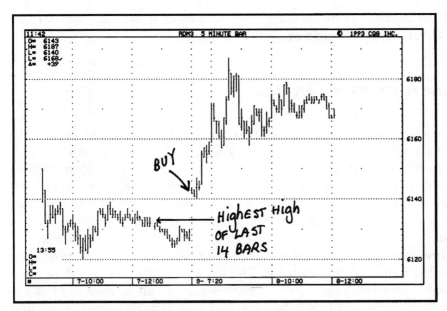

Figure 11-1. 14-period channel breakout above resistance (highs).

Figure 11-2. 14-period channel breakout below support (lows).

speak for themselves by showing you some system test results generated with Omega research program TradeStation.

How the Channel Breakout System Works

The *channel breakout system (CBO)* is a very simple system indeed. In fact, it's as old as the hills, dating back to the days of "old man" Keltner who published the Keltner Statistical Service on commodities back in the 1950s and 1960s. The idea is quite logical and elementary. In fact it's beautiful in its simplicity. It is based on the fact that markets spend most of their time moving sideways as opposed to trending. When such a sideways pattern, or channel, develops, the astute trader will want to buy breakouts above the top of the channel while selling breakouts below the bottom of the channel. The logic is solid; however, one must remember that there are many false breakouts. This is why the CBO is not an especially accurate technique and why it is, however, a method which can pinpoint the start of major intraday moves.

Here are the simple CBO rules of application:

Channel Breakout Rules and Methods

1. Determine the length of the CBO channel in terms of price bars. In other words, if you are using a 14-period length, you will watch the last 14 price bars previous to the current price bar for a buy or sell signal.

2. If you are using a 14-day period then a *buy signal* will occur when the high of the current bar exceeds the highest high of the previous 14 price bars by x number of ticks. In most cases the x is defined as one or two ticks.

3. If you are using a 14-day period then a *sell signal* will occur when the low of the current bar is lower than the lowest low of the previous 14 price bars by x number of ticks. In most cases the x is defined as one or two ticks.

4. Risk or stop loss can be defined in many ways, or the system can be used as a reversing system.

5. The CBO method tests extremely well on daily data and has considerable potential on intraday data as well.

```
Consecutive Closes  SP E92-10 min   01/02/92 - 12/31/92
                    Performance Summary:  All Trades

Total net profit        $  18300.00   Open position P/L       $      0.00
Gross profit            $  61900.00   Gross loss              $ -43600.00

Total # of trades             169     Percent profitable            56%
Number winning trades          95     Number losing trades          74

Largest winning trade   $   2975.00   Largest losing trade    $  -2000.00
Average winning trade   $    651.58   Average losing trade    $   -589.19
Ratio avg win/avg loss         1.11   Avg trade(win & loss)   $    108.28

Max consec. winners             7     Max consec. losers             8
Avg # bars in winners          20     Avg # bars in losers          20

Max intraday drawdown   $  -7925.00
Profit factor                  1.42   Max # contracts held           1
Account size required   $  10925.00   Return on account           168%


                    Performance Summary:  Long Trades

Total net profit        $  14775.00   Open position P/L       $      0.00
Gross profit            $  35025.00   Gross loss              $ -20250.00

Total # of trades              97     Percent profitable            65%
Number winning trades          63     Number losing trades          34

Largest winning trade   $   2500.00   Largest losing trade    $  -2000.00
Average winning trade   $    555.95   Average losing trade    $   -595.59
Ratio avg win/avg loss         0.93   Avg trade(win & loss)   $    152.32

Max consec. winners             8     Max consec. losers             4
Avg # bars in winners          18     Avg # bars in losers          18

Max intraday drawdown   $  -3575.00
Profit factor                  1.73   Max # contracts held           1
Account size required   $   6575.00   Return on account           225%


                    Performance Summary:  Short Trades

Total net profit        $   3525.00   Open position P/L       $      0.00
Gross profit            $  26875.00   Gross loss              $ -23350.00

Total # of trades              72     Percent profitable            44%
Number winning trades          32     Number losing trades          40

Largest winning trade   $   2975.00   Largest losing trade    $  -1475.00
Average winning trade   $    839.84   Average losing trade    $   -583.75
Ratio avg win/avg loss         1.44   Avg trade(win & loss)   $     48.96

Max consec. winners             3     Max consec. losers             5
Avg # bars in winners          24     Avg # bars in losers          21

Max intraday drawdown   $  -6850.00
Profit factor                  1.15   Max # contracts held           1
Account size required   $   9850.00   Return on account            36%
```

Figure 11-3. System test results—intraday channel breakout in S&P futures.

The CBO method was tested on TradeStation with good results. Figure 11-3 shows performance of the CBO system with the indicated parameters in S&P futures.

Summary and Conclusions

The CBO system is a sound and useful one for day traders. Its rules of application are specific, objective, and mechanical. It is readily tracked by computer and tends to get on board when major moves occur within the day time frame. I recommend tracking this method in the more active markets, particularly those markets which have a high dollar value per tick. As with most day-trade systems discussed in this book, entry signals are specific and objective. Exiting positions, however, are less objective, and you may wish to close out positions by allowing yourself to either be stopped out using a close trailing stop loss, or you may wish to exit at a given price or time target. It is not uncommon for large profits to be diminished substantially as a result of waiting for a reversing signal.

12

Traditional Methods of Technical Analysis and Day Trading

Since traditional technical analysis has been so popular for so many years, many futures traders are very familiar with the application of such principles as chart formations, trend line penetrations, price patterns, and the many different methods of interpretation associated with these formations. Many of these patterns have been used with great success by traders over the years; however, there has been a steadily growing belief in recent years that these chart patterns are not necessarily reliable and that they are, in many cases, subject to considerable interpretation. Traders who claim to be objective and scientific reject any method or trading technique which cannot be fully tested.

Clearly, the primary cause of the growing tide of counter-chart-analysis sentiment is that many of the chart formations and patterns cannot be fully or thoroughly tested by computer. Nor can hypothetical results be sufficiently quantified to instill the degree of confidence which so many contemporary traders demand. My personal opinion on this matter, as you may well have gathered from my comments throughout this text, is that computer testing is considerably overrated and that, in the final analysis, it does not necessarily guarantee profitable results.

I have deemphasized the value of computer testing and reemphasized the value of individual trader's skill as a critical variable in the formula for profitable day trading. In fact, it is certainly not an unacceptable extrapolation to extend these comments to all types of trading. With this in mind, *I cannot include myself among the many who denigrate the value of traditional technical indicators.* I believe that there are many short-term and day-trading tools which are derived from traditional chart analysis. This book is not intended to serve as a compendium of traditional tools applied to day trading. So many excellent books have been written on the subject that anything I could add might be redundant. I will spend just a little time, however, illustrating some of the methods to you so that you may make your own decisions and/or be prompted to do your own research, whatever form that may take.

The most supportive aspect of traditional chart analysis for day trading rests in the fact that many day traders on the exchange floor use traditional chart indicators in their trading. Experience and keen observation have taught me to be a traditionalist with respect to market analysis and trading.

Although this may seem, to many of you, to be incompatible with the tasks and objectives of the day trader, my work suggests that there may be many profitable opportunities to apply traditional charting principles in the day trading. *As long as you are the type of individual who is willing to accept visual evidence as opposed to hard scientific validation, then this chapter may be very helpful to you.* If, however, hard science and definitive answers are what you seek, then I suggest you skip this chapter and move onto something else.

Trend Line Analysis

A *trend line* is a straight line which connects significant tops or bottoms on a chart in order to illustrate support or resistance points.

A support line is one which connects chart lows.

A resistance line is one which connects chart highs.

A minimum of three points are required to produce a valid trend line. I do not mean to insult your intelligence if you are already familiar with trend lines (which is probably true for the vast majority of you).

Figure 12-1 shows a number of support and resistance trend lines. Although there are no firm statistics on the effectiveness of trend line usage, I've found trend lines to be very effective for intraday trading using 5-, 10-, and 20-minute charts.

Trend lines may be used as follows:

- *Buying at support.* This is a simple procedure. Once support has been established, buy when prices decline to support in an up trend. Figure 12-1 illustrates this approach.

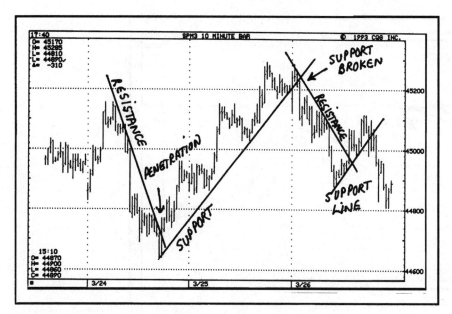

Figure 12-1. Support and resistance trend lines on intraday chart.

- *Selling at resistance.* Also a simple method, this approach sells at a resistance trend line in a down trend once resistance has been established. Figure 12-1 illustrates this approach.

- *Selling breakouts below support.* Once support has been established, a decline below support (breakout down) is considered a sign of weakness, i.e., a break in the trend, and used for the purpose of selling out existing long positions or for establishing short positions. See Figure 12-2.

- *Buying breakouts above resistance.* Once resistance has been established, a move above resistance (breakout up) is considered a sign of strength, i.e., a break in the trend, and used for the purpose of buying back existing short positions or for establishing new long positions. See Figure 12-3.

When determining trend lines it is often helpful to go back several days in order to determine the location of the line. But do not get carried away by attempting to trace a trend line back several weeks using intraday data—there is no reason to do this. Several days, even one day, will be sufficient.

Figure 12-2. Support, resistance, and trends.

Figure 12-3. Support, resistance, and intraday signals.

Trend Line Applications—Chart Formations

As I've indicated above, I feel that the use of trend lines, although seen by many as too simple, can, in fact, be a very effective day-trading method. Many very large intraday price moves have given trend line signals. I recommend the use of trend line analysis as both an effective as well as time-tested method. While there is clearly some art to the science of trend line analysis, it is a technique which few traders use during these days of high-tech trading.

Flags and Pennants. A flag or pennant chart formation is exactly what its name implies. Figure 12-4 shows a few flags on intraday charts. As you can see, the narrowing portion of a flag usually develops into a breakout up or down. The trader using such formations will be alert to the possibility of a breakout as the flag narrows, and he or she will trade with the direction of the breakout.

Rounding Tops, Rounding Bottoms. Yet another classical chart formation is the rounding top or bottom. Figures 12-5 and 12-6 show such patterns on intraday charts. Day traders will want to sell short or exit long positions when the lowest portion of the rounding top has

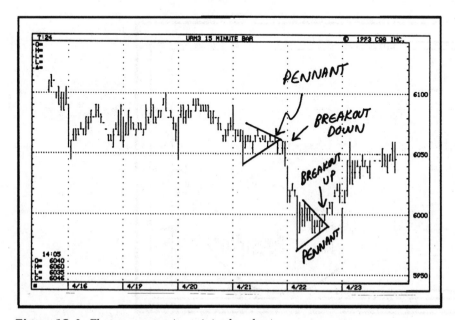

Figure 12-4. Flags or pennants on intraday chart.

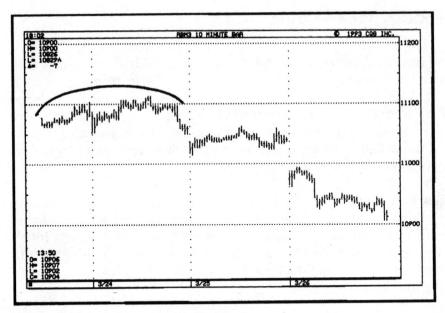

Figure 12-5. Rounding top on intraday chart.

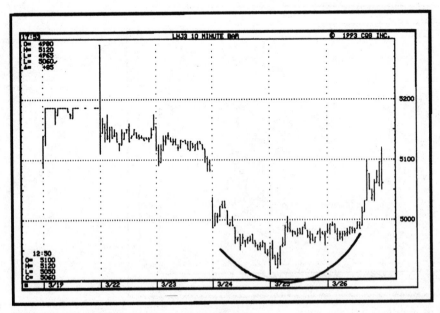

Figure 12-6. Rounding bottom on intraday chart.

been penetrated. Day traders will want to buy when the highest portion of the rounding bottom has been penetrated. In practice such formations are rather rare on intraday charts. Study intraday charts and see how many of these formations you can spot.

Breakaway Gaps. Typically such a pattern is a good one; however, the majority of research on such gaps has been on daily price charts. In practice, breakaway gaps rarely occur on intraday charts. Figure 12-7 shows such a formation. Chartists feel that such gaps, if in the up direction, are very bullish and, if in the down direction, are very bearish.

Key Reversals. A key reversal up occurs when a market trades below the low of its last price bar, above the high of its last price bar, and closes above the close of its last price bar. My research has shown such patterns not to be too effective on daily bar charts, but they appear to be much more significant on intraday charts. Figure 12-8 shows such a formation and its consequence.

A key reversal down occurs when the market trades above its last price bar, below its last price bar, and then closes below the close of its last price bar. Figure 12-9 shows such a formation.

Reversals tend to be good signals for day trading, apparently much better than they are for short-term or position trading.

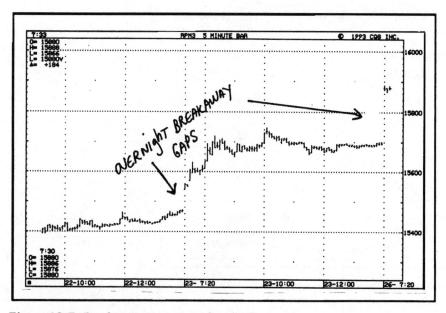

Figure 12-7. Breakaway gap on intraday chart.

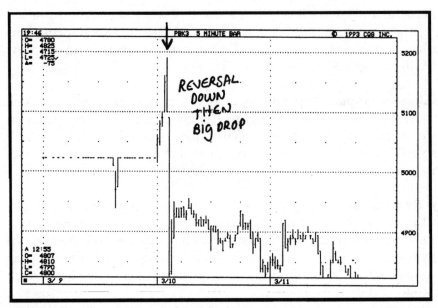

Figure 12-8. Reversal down on intraday chart.

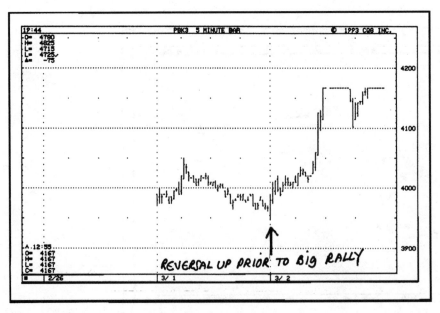

Figure 12-9. Reversal up on intraday chart.

Congestion and Breakouts. These are very important patterns on intraday charts. Congestion occurs when prices trade within a very well defined range either after a rally or a decline or within an existing period of strength or weakness. Figure 12-10 shows a few examples of price congestion. They also show what occurs after a breakout from congestion. As you can see, breakouts following periods of congestion can be very profitable within the day time frame. I recommend you follow them. While this is not a totally mechanical methodology, it is not difficult to use and can yield large rewards. It does take some training and experience, however.

Summary and Conclusions

Although some traders will criticize the use of chart patterns as lacking the kind of objectivity required in this day and age of computerized trading, I do not agree. I feel that the skilled chartist can trade much more profitably than can the pure technician. It is, however, much more difficult to become skilled at recognizing and using chart patterns than it is to read a simple technical indicator. But in order to do so the trader

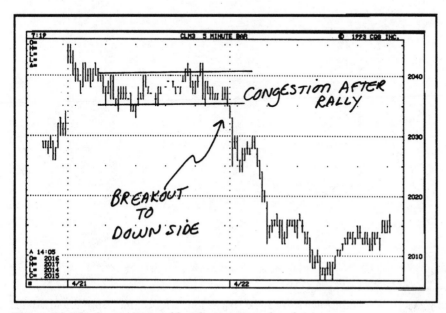

Figure 12-10. Congestion and breakout on intraday chart.

will need to have considerable experience, experience which can only be acquired through practice, practice, and more practice. Therefore, my advice to would-be chartists who plan to use their skills for day trading is to become very familiar with the patterns described above and with those described in the standard technical analysis texts such as Edwards and McGee.[*]

---

[*]R. D. Edwards and J. McGee, *Technical Analysis of Stock Trends*, John McGee, Inc., Springfield, Mass., 1966.

13

A Unique Oscillator for Day Trading

An oscillator is a timing indicator which is comprised essentially of two or more moving averages. To *oscillate* means to move back and forth between extremes. Hence, an oscillator is an indicator which changes values between two extreme levels. The stochastic indicator is an oscillator, and so are RSI, MOM, and ROC. Not all oscillators are the same even though they are based on the same general idea. The basic construction of a two-line oscillator appears as shown in Figure 13-1. As you can see, the oscillator values generate buy and sell signals when they change their positions by crossing over one another. The simplest oscillator consists of two moving averages.

Such indicators as the moving average convergence-divergence (MACD) consist of exponential moving averages which generate buy and sell signals when they cross, very similar to the relationships shown in Figure 13-1.

Although MACD is a very effective technique for day trading, there is another oscillator method which I feel has more potential for the day trader. MACD, in my experience, is a very effective method for trading short-term price swings of from 2 to 6 days' duration.

Figures 13-2 and 13-3 illustrate how MACD buy and sell signals occur on the intraday S&P futures charts. As you can see, MACD is an outstanding indicator for trading such moves. MACD is also an acceptable indicator for day trading, but I find that another oscillator is preferable. Specifically, I am referring to an oscillator which compares opening to closing prices on an intraday basis.

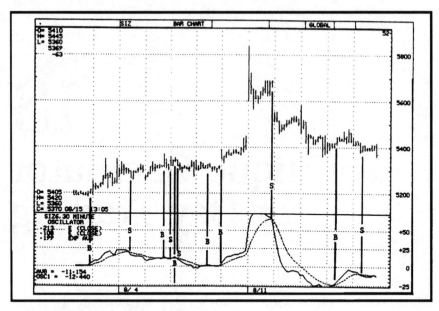

Figure 13-1. Ideal MACD oscillator signals.

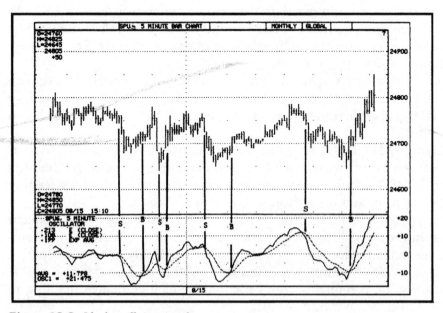

Figure 13-2. Ideal oscillator signals.

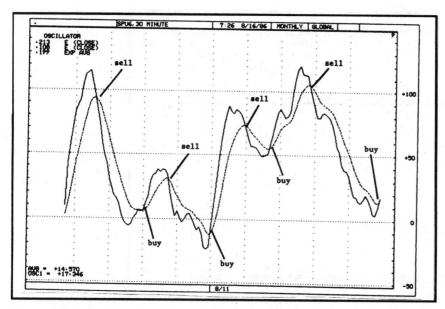

Figure 13-3. MACD signals used in short-term trading.

Opens versus Closes

Although there is no such thing as a 5-minute open or a 5-minute close, the concept is a simple one to understand. The first price tick of a 5-minute period is arbitrarily defined as the open, and the last tick of the 5-minute time segment is arbitrarily defined as the 5-minute close.

The relationship is a simple one. It is based on the well-established pattern for closing prices in a bull trend to be higher than opening prices and for closing prices in a bear trend to be lower than opening prices. By comparing a moving average of the 5-, 10-, or 15-minute openings with a moving average of the 5-, 10-, or 15-minute closings, we can quickly detect trend changes either before they occur or very early in their inception.

Figures 13-4a and 13-4b illustrate the ideal signals and relationship to which I am referring using a 5-minute chart of S&P futures. Examine my buy and sell signals in relation to price trend changes during the day. Figure 13-5 shows the same oscillator combination and signals on a Swiss franc chart.

As you can see from the illustrations, the signals are very reliable and tend to signal major moves. I call this method the O/C oscillator (O/C). Although the O/C method is wonderful for catching large intraday price swings, it does have its limitations which I will discuss later on.

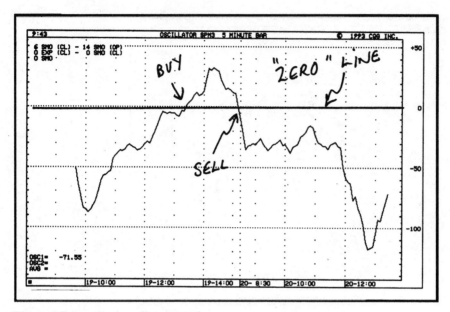

Figure 13-4a. Ideal oscillator signals.

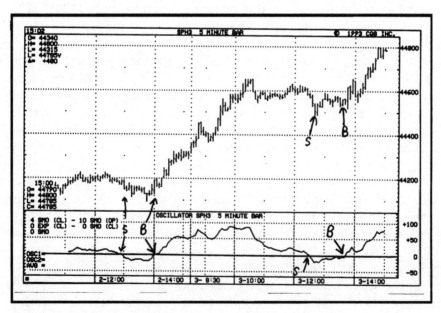

Figure 13-4b. Open and close oscillator signals in 5-minute S&P.

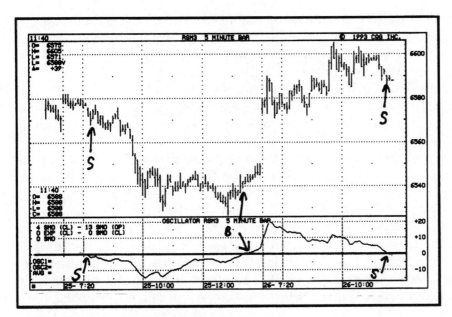

Figure 13-5. Open and close oscillator signals in 5-minute Swiss francs.

Before doing so, however, I'll review the construction of the O/C oscillator, and then I'll give you rules for using it.

Construction of the O/C for Intraday Trading

The O/C is constructed as follows:

1. Use two smoothed moving averages (MAs) as follows:
   a. A smoothed moving average of the opening prices consisting of 6 to 10 periods on 5-, 10-, 15-, or 20-minute data.
   b. A second smoothed moving average which consists of closing prices of 12 to 24 periods on 5-, 10-, 15-, or 20-minute data.
2. Buy and sell on crossovers of the two MA lines. When the MA of the close crosses over the MA of the open, a buy is signaled, and when the MA of the close falls below the MA of the open, a sell is signaled.
3. You will need to adjust the lengths used as a function of the time span you are using (i.e., 5-, 10-, 15-, or 20-minute data) and the volatility of the market you are following. There are no hard and fast rules for doing this. You will need to use your judgment; however, after you work with this method for a while, you will become quite adept at making the proper selections. (Formula for smoothed MA is in appendix at end of book.)

4. An important issue which you will need to deal with is the amount of the crossover. In other words, you will need to determine how much of a crossover will be sufficient to generate a signal in either direction. In this respect consider Figure 13-6. As you can see, the minor crossovers, which do occur, are not reliable. They must be sufficiently large. You will need to determine the crossover amount or threshold. You can do this fairly easily be examining recent signals. Be sure to monitor the O/C performance closely.

5. You may use O/C signals in the opposite direction to reverse positions, or you may use a trailing stop loss to exit prior to a reversing signal. Some subjective decisions may be necessary in exiting trades which are initiated using O/C signals, but I stress that this is *not a totally mechanical system*. It does require decisions. It is, however, one of the most sensitive methods I know for trading volatile markets such as S&P and the currencies. It has also worked well in other markets. Naturally, you will want to be out of all trades by the end of the day, and you will wait for the next day to enter on new signals.

Examining Some Signals

Figures 13-7 through 13-11 illustrate O/C signals in a number of markets using various time lengths along with my hand-written comments.

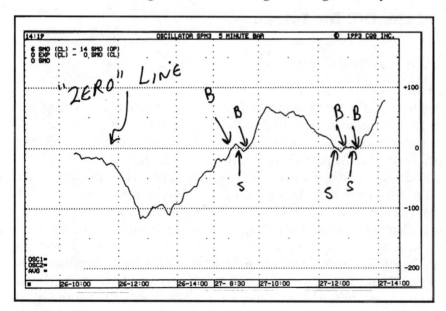

Figure 13-6. O/C false signals.

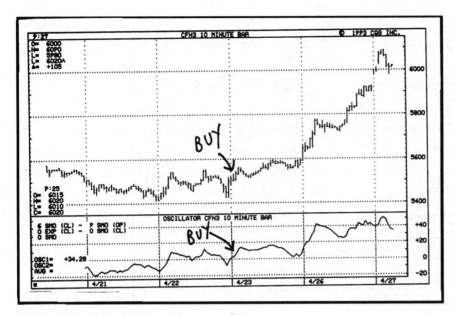

Figure 13-7. O/C signals on 10-minute data.

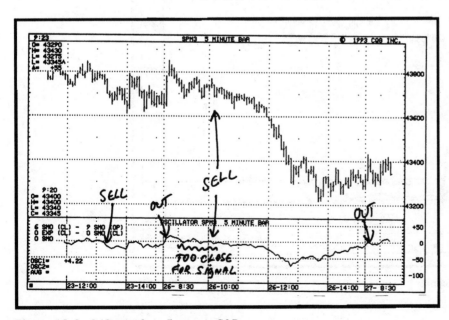

Figure 13-8. O/C signals in 5-minute S&P.

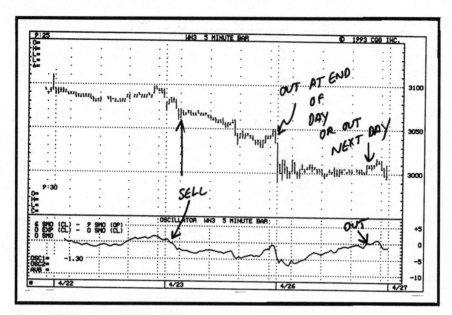

Figure 13-9. O/C signals in 5-minute wheat.

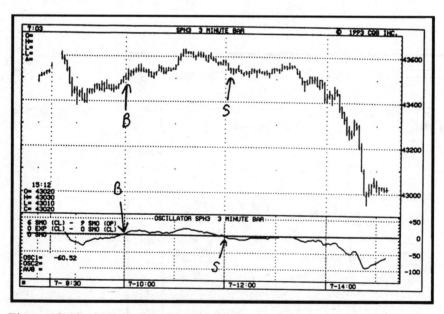

Figure 13-10. O/C signals in 3-minute S&P.

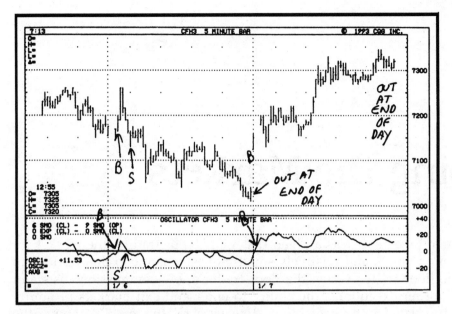

Figure 13-11. O/C signals in 5-minute coffee.

Summary and Conclusions

The O/C system is a sound and useful one for day traders. Its rules of application for entry signals are specific, objective, and mechanical. It is readily tracked by computer and tends to get on board when major moves occur within the day time frame. I recommend tracking this method in the more active markets, particularly those markets which have a high dollar value per tick. As with most day-trade systems discussed in this book, entry signals are specific and objective. Exiting positions, however, are less objective. This method, in particular, is amenable to the use of a fairly close trailing stop-loss. You may wish to exit at a given price or time target. It is not uncommon for large profits to be diminished substantially as a result of waiting for a reversing signal.

Yet another suggested method of exit is to use a shorter-term time frame for exit than was originally used for entry. If you use an entry signal generated on a 10-minute S&P chart, you could exit when the 3- or 5-minute S&P chart gave its subsequent reversal signal. At this point you would not reverse position, you would merely close the position out. This, by the way, is an excellent method for exiting positions using other timing signals than the O/C.

14
Scalping the Markets

For many years, it was a given that *scalping,* or trading the market for extremely quick and relatively small moves, was the exclusive domain of the floor trader. Given the floor trader's low commission costs and quick order executions, the ability to enter and exit markets promptly was translated into profitable trading with relative ease. Although the scalping game has become more competitive in recent years, it is still a game which may be played with fairly good odds of success provided one is acquainted with the proper techniques.

Unfortunately, many futures traders do not understand how the majority of floor traders operate. This misunderstanding, or I should say lack of understanding, leads to the erroneous conclusion that we, as off-the-floor traders, somehow compete directly with traders on the floor. This is not necessarily true. *What suits the floor trader in terms of technique and goal is not necessarily right for the outside or off-the-floor trader.* The majority of floor traders prefer to trade markets which move in fairly narrow but well-defined price ranges, thereby allowing them to buy and sell frequently, trading large positions for small moves. *In other words, most floor traders are perfectly content to trade back and forth in a market, taking profits of one or two ticks frequently during the course of each trading day.* What the floor trader misses in size of price move is easily compensated for in size of position. Whereas the average off-the-floor trader seeks to profit from fairly large moves, the floor trader seeks to profit from small moves using large positions.

Given the general availability of instant price quotations, computerized trading systems, and low commission costs, it is possible for all traders to become scalpers, assuming that they have the temperament and motivation to do so. But I warn you that of all the possible day-trading methods and orientations, scalping is the most demanding, the most intense, and the most difficult to learn. Yet it is paradoxically simple in its goals and intentions. Before discussing some of my favorite scalping techniques, I'll first define both the goal of scalping and how scalpers do what they do.

What Is Scalping?

Although the term *scalping* most likely originated in the heritage of the wild, wild American West, the contemporary trend for outrage at the mere mention of ethnic issues prompts me to side-step the derivation of this term. Simply stated, *the scalper attempts to trade futures markets for only several ticks, taking advantage of fairly narrow trading ranges in order to "buy the bid and sell the offer."* The scalper, who is usually a floor trader, attempts to capitalize on relatively quiet times in the markets, buying at the prevailing price (the bid price) or hopefully at one or two ticks below the anticipated fair price and selling at a slightly higher price or what is called the *offer price.* The best way I can drive home the point of what it is that scalpers do is to state succinctly that *scalpers attempt to buy at wholesale and sell at retail.*

As you can understand, the price markup from wholesale to retail, although very high in some businesses, is not too high in the scalping business. Frequently, the markup amounts to only one or two price ticks. However, at $30 or more per price tick in Treasury bond futures, the prospects for profitable scalping are considerable. If the trader is paying very small commissions ($14 or lower per trade), then a good portion of each price tick per contract is profit. What the scalper may give up in the way of price movement, he or she can compensate for in terms of position size. From the scalper's point of view, a trade of two ticks' profit on 500 contracts works out to 1000 ticks—1000 ticks after approximately $15 in costs (which is a very high cost for the floor trader) works out to roughly $16,000 profit. Assuming a commission rate of $8 and often much, much lower for the floor trader, the profits are even more substantial.

It is now possible for traders who are not on the floor of the various exchanges to trade in a fashion very similar to what floor traders do when they scalp the markets. Using some of the techniques discussed in this book, the average trader who is willing to sit at the computer screen and watch the market tick-by-tick all day long can scalp in a fashion similar to floor traders. During the last few years, many floor traders, realizing that scalping is possible without being on the floor of the exchange, have left to become *upstairs traders.* An upstairs trader trades as if he or she were on the floor but is, in actuality, trading from an office, usually located in the exchange building.

Rules for Scalping

In order to scalp the markets effectively, you must apply certain rules which do not necessarily apply to other forms of day trading. You will need to know and observe these rules carefully and consistently if you plan to become a successful scalper:

1. *To compensate for the relatively small size of moves* which you will attempt to be capturing as a scalper, you will need to trade considerably larger positions.

2. *If you are not willing to accept the risk of trading larger positions,* then you cannot scalp the markets in a fashion which makes trading worth your while. After all, if you plan to scalp bonds for one or two ticks at a time three or four times a day, and if you are unsuccessful in your efforts one or two times a day, then the bottom line of your trading on a one-contract basis may only be one tick. Subtracting from this commission costs, your scalping will prove to be a losing proposition or a minimally profitable venture, above and beyond what you have lost in terms of time. Therefore, it is necessary for you to make a commitment to larger positions, perhaps 5 or 10 contracts at a time, and to increase your position size once you have mastered the various scalping techniques I will suggest in this chapter.

3. *To be a successful scalper, you will need to take your losses as well as your profits very quickly.* If, for example, you are long T-bonds at $105.20 expecting a move to $105.22, then you must enter orders to sell at $105.22, since you have set yourself a two-tick target. To expect $105.23 or $105.24 would not be consistent with your scalping goals. The idea is to take numerous small profits of several ticks on large positions throughout the day. Only by following this goal will you achieve success as a scalper.

4. You must pay close attention to the market you are trading at all times. This means that you will be able to trade only one market at a time, since you will need to be at the screen watching every tick. If you have a multiple screen monitor, it may be possible to scalp more than one market at a time; however, I think that pragmatically this would be difficult. In addition to these rules, which are more operational rather than methodological, important techniques are explained in the next section.

Suggested Methods of Scalping

To scalp a market effectively, you must first isolate a specific trading range which is clearly defined in terms of support and resistance or in terms of bid and offer. As you know, the bid price is the price at which buyers are willing to buy; the offer price is a price at which sellers are willing to sell. In most cases, there is a spread, or difference between the two, sometimes of one tick in size and other times several ticks in size, depending upon the market. In Treasury bonds, the bid offer spread is usually one tick. Therefore, by knowing the bid and the offer, the scalper will attempt to buy at the bid price and sell at the offer price, otherwise known as buying the bid and selling the offer.

Here is a suggested technique for taking advantage of the bid-offer spread. Assume that Treasury bond futures have been trading in a fairly narrow trading range after the initial opening volatility has been digested. The market begins to trade between $103.15 and $103.17, a two-tick range. As long as the market continues to trade in this range (and this could change at virtually any time), you will want to buy at the lower end of the range and sell at the higher end of the range. In order to do this, you will enter specific price orders to buy at $103.15. Fill-or-kill orders should be used wherever possible. Therefore, you will enter an order, for example, to buy March 1993 bonds at $105.15 fill or kill. Within several minutes, you will know whether you have been filled. If you have been filled, you will then enter an opposite order to sell, perhaps at $105.16 or $105.17 which is within the asking price range.

This is the very basic technique of buying at the bid and selling at the offer. As you can see, it is considerably more difficult to do off the floor than it is on the trading floor, since floor traders know immediately whether they have been filled without having to wait for a third party to confirm the price execution. The on-the-floor trader can, therefore, trade with much greater speed than can the off-the-floor trader, who must await confirmation of order fills. Depending upon the firm with which you are doing business, the use of fill-or-kill orders may, if used too frequently, alienate brokers as well as floor traders. Therefore, the fill-or-kill order should be used only when absolutely necessary or in cases where the firm you are dealing with has no objections.

Another technique would be to use a price order and to give the market sufficient time to fill your order. In this case, I recommend working with a brokerage firm that will report your fills back to you as quickly as possible. The problem with scalping away from the pit is not knowing whether you have been filled.

Moving Average Channels

One of the methods described earlier in this book, the MAC (moving average channel) lends itself readily to use by scalpers. My recommended parameters for the MAC are 10 units of the high and 8 units of the low. For scalpers these parameters are likely to be somewhat long. I recommend instead using 5 units of the high and 4 units of the low.

Figure 14-1 illustrates how the MAC will look in relation to 5-minute price bars in T-bond futures. Figures 14-2 and 14-3 illustrate the same methodology in Swiss francs and S&P futures.

These illustrations are included here merely as examples, but they are fairly typical in terms of structure and clearly show that scalping the market by buying the low of the channel and exiting at the high of the channel in an up trend is a good procedure. Conversely, in a down trend, you may scalp the market by selling the high of the channel and buying the low of the channel.

Alternatively, in sideways trending markets, the procedure is to buy the low of the channel, reversing position and selling the high of the channel, and then reversing position again by covering shorts at the low of the channel and going long.

Ideally, this technique will work in any market which has established some specific channel relationships. It is your job to identify markets which are suitable for scalping. I have included several more examples which will help you identify the types of markets you want to trade for scalping purposes. *Remember that as a scalper it is your job to exit profitable and losing positions quickly in order to capitalize on the many price swings*

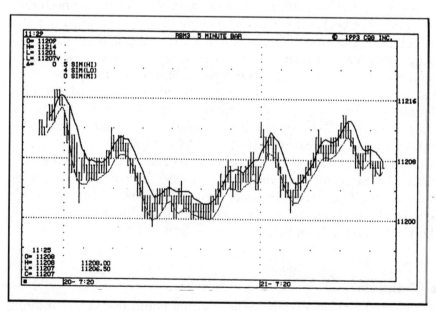

Figure 14-1. The 5/4 MAC and 5-minute T-bond futures.

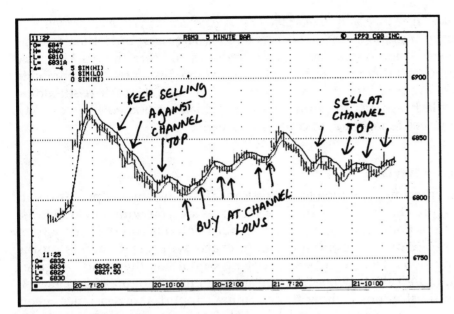

Figure 14-2. The 5/4 MAC and 5-minute Swiss franc futures.

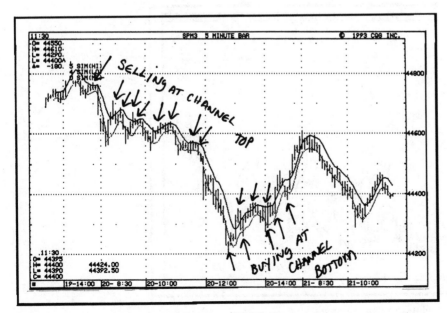

Figure 14-3. The 5/4 MAC and 5-minute S&P futures.

each day. It is especially important to exit your losing positions promptly so that your small profits will not be erased by one large loss. Unfortunately, this happens all too often. Sadly, some traders will scalp the markets very effectively all day long, only to allow one large losing trade to eliminate their entire profit for the day or worse. Therefore, the scalper should be particularly attuned to exiting positions which are not working, quickly, without hesitation, and, of course, decisively.

Point-and-Figure Charting

Another technique which lends itself readily to use by scalpers is point-and-figure charting. This book cannot provide you with a detailed discussion of point-and-figure charting, but I will tell you that many floor traders I know use point-and-figure charts with great success on the trading floor. Their charts are kept up to date as they trade. Figures 14-4 and 14-5 show two sample intraday point and figure charts as well as my illustrations of how to determine support and resistance levels for the purpose of buying and selling. Also, I recommend reading several of the excellent point-and-figure texts available. Here are some suggestions:

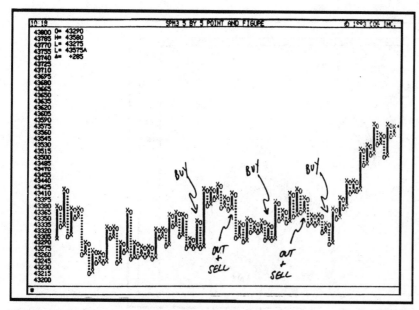

Figure 14-4. Intraday point-and-figure signals.

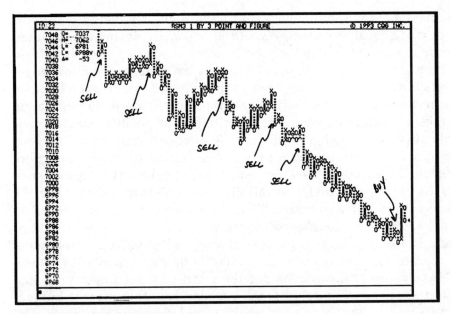

Figure 14-5. Intraday point-and-figure signals.

The Market Profile

The market profile is yet another technique which can be used for the purpose of scalping. J. Peter Steidlmayer, developer of the technique in association with the Chicago Board of Trade, has published many fine articles and several books on the topic. In addition, Dalton and Jones published *Mind over Money*, which describes their adaptation of the market profile technique in great detail. Since the market profile is an extremely detailed and extensive topic, I will not discuss it herein, but I will tell you that if you understand the profile you can use it very successfully for the purpose of day trading. Of particular importance in using the profile is the TPO count and the concept of market balance. The best type of day for trading for scalping the market is what Steidlmayer identifies as the *normal distribution day*. As I noted earlier, I suggest you read any of the excellent references available on the market profile such as Pete's excellent books or *Mind over Money* (Probus Books, Chicago, 1989) by Dalton and Jones.

Scalping on Rising or Falling Markets

I have not yet said enough about the procedures for scalping within existing trends. Although most scalpers can do extremely well in sideways markets which move back and forth regularly between support and resistance, scalpers can also profit handsomely during quick moves either up or down. Such moves tend to occur most often after the release of certain government reports, statements by supposedly knowledgeable officials, or international news events. Should you happen to be on the correct side of a market which begins to move sharply in your favor, then take advantage of the move by exiting your position immediately. It is always easier to exit a position while prices are moving within your favor than it is to do so when prices have started to change direction. Therefore, the successful scalper will want to take advantage of such *bulges,* or *craters,* as I prefer to call them, by entering orders while the market is still moving in your favor. *Do not wait until the trend has either slowed, lost momentum, or changed direction.*

There is a certain degree of tape-reading skill involved in following such a procedure; however, it can certainly be developed with experience. As an illustration, consider the chart and accompanying tick printout shown in Figure 14-6. As you can see, this market bulged, began to trend sharply higher, peaked, and then turned lower. The scalper who took advantage of the bulge to exit per my illustrations did well. However, the scalper who failed to do so did not profit handsomely at all.

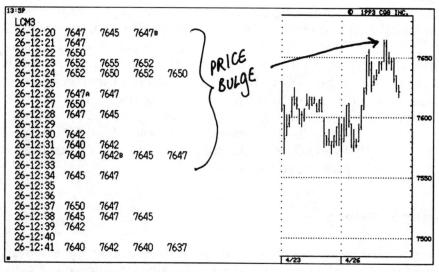

Figure 14-6. Tick data—time and sales.

Summary

Scalpers find themselves in a unique category of day traders. Not only do they seek to trade within the day time frame, but they also attempt to capitalize on the most minute of moves during the day. In order to be a successful scalper, you must either possess or develop specific skills to assist you in your endeavors. Since the scalper seeks to profit only on extremely small moves of several price ticks, it is of paramount importance that positions be entered and exited quickly and that trading be done on a large scale in order to compensate for the relatively small size of price moves. The scalper who truly wishes to be successful must be willing to trade large positions, to take small moves out of the market, and to do so many times each day. While I feel that in some ways the job of the scalper is more well-defined and more easily implemented than that of the more traditional day trader, it is also an extremely demanding role inasmuch as large positions which move against the scalper quickly can prove very costly. Therefore, if you intend to be a scalper, begin to increase your position size slowly and do so only as a function of your financial ability.

Buying into Large Declines or Selling into Large Rallies

Many traders feel that they can successfully scalp a few ticks out of a market by buying into large price declines in bull trends or selling into large price rallies in bear trends. This certainly makes a great deal of sense in terms of ideal thinking; however, in practice it is a very risky procedure because large price declines can continue well beyond theoretical support levels and large price rallies in existing bear trends can continue well beyond theoretical resistance points. Nevertheless, very quick money can be made during such moves. The scalper can take advantage of these, provided certain rules are followed.

First, I refer you to my book *Short-term Trading in Futures* (Probus Publishing, Chicago, 1988) for additional methods of support and resistance trading on a short-term basis. In particular, consult the section on price spikes and probes. These two techniques, namely buying on probes to support and selling on probes to resistance, can prove very effective to the scalper who is willing to establish a position during large declines to support or large rallies to resistance but who must also be willing to exit these positions very quickly, right or wrong. An illustration will serve to clarify what I am suggesting. If you will recall my discussion of price spikes and probes, I noted that when a market declines quickly to a previous price spike on the down side that very quick rallies can develop within a matter of seconds or minutes. This is particularly advantageous to the scalper who will anticipate such moves; moves which usually occur in response to significant government reports or other scheduled news items.

Conclusions

No matter what method you use for scalping the futures markets, remember that the scalper attempts to achieve the following important goals:

1. To trade as often as possible to accumulate as much profit as possible by taking advantage of small but reliable moves within the day time frame

2. To exit positions very quickly either at a profit or at a loss

3. To avoid having a strong opinion as to market direction in order to limit the possibility of being influenced to act on opinion as opposed to market fact

15

The Importance
of Orders

To the day trader (in fact to all traders), using the right price order is just as important as using the right tool for the right job is to the mechanic or carpenter. Using the right orders can spell the difference between profits and losses. Using a market order when a stop or stop limit order should have been used may result in a poor price fill which will cost you dollars. Since the bottom line is very important to day traders, perhaps more important than to any other type of trader other than a scalper (who is also a day trader), every tick saved is indeed a tick earned. Orders should be specifically geared to what you seek to achieve in terms of your timing your trading system. Orders are designed to save you money, not to lose you money. They will help you reduce bad fills and avoid lost points or price skids. But to use price orders to your advantage, you must be familiar with the various types of orders and when they are best used. You must also know what orders to avoid and when to avoid them.

What You Should Know about Market Orders

Market orders must be avoided whenever possible. A market order is, as far as I'm concerned, a license to steal. Rarely will a market order be filled at the exact price you are expecting. Typically, a market order will cost you one tick, at times two or three. In S&P futures, a market order may cost you much more than just a few ticks, although one or two ticks in a quiet market is not unusual. If you lose two ticks on entry and two ticks on exit, the cost per trade will most assuredly add up. However, not using market orders will cause you to risk not getting a position at all or not being able to exit a position at all. Here are some guidelines for using market orders:

- *Only use a market order when absolutely necessary.* If you are using an intraday oscillator type signal which enters at the end of a given time segment, then a market order is acceptable. If, however, you can use a specific price order as opposed to a market order, this is preferable. It is not uncommon for markets to make a quick move following a signal, but very often the market returns to its original entry price fairly soon, and a price order would have been sufficient. You can save a great deal of money this way.

- *If you are riding a fairly large profit* and wish to exit a position quickly since your indicators have turned, then it is worth giving some of the profit back just to make sure you are out of your position.

- *Avoid market-on-close* (MOC) orders. All too often such orders are even more of a license to steal, since they can be filled at almost any price during the last minute of trading. An MOC order in thin markets is a certain invitation to trouble. Avoid MOC orders unless absolutely necessary. Many traders jokingly refer to MOCs as "murder-on-close" orders, since fills are often so poor.

- *Never use market orders with spreads.* You are far better off using specific spread levels for entry and exit, or you may use specific price orders in each market individually to "leg" into or out of the spread. Considerable slippage is the rule in spread market orders. Unfortunately the only orders you can use in spreads are market orders or price orders. Of the two types, price orders are clearly preferable.

Market-If-Touched (MIT) Orders

An MIT order to buy is always placed below the market, and an MIT order to sell is placed above the market. An MIT order becomes a market order when hit. Therefore, if you have an MIT order to buy at 4150 this order will become a market order as soon as a trade occurs at 4150. The pit broker holding this order will immediately buy at the market. You could get filled at any price; however, you will usually be filled at or near your order, at times better than your price and at times worse. This is the chance you take when using such an order. An MIT order is used when you have a specific price level in mind for entry and you do not wish to take the chance of not being filled. Ordinarily such orders are used for selling at resistance above the market for buying at support below the market.

The day trader who is using the support and resistance methods described in this book may use MIT orders; however, do note that such orders can cost you a few ticks. MITs are, however, excellent orders to use when trading support and resistance levels. Remember that such orders are not accepted by all exchanges nor are they accepted at all times. Under certain market conditions MIT orders may be refused at the discretion either of the pit broker or of the exchange.

Fill-or-Kill (FOK) Orders

A fill-or-kill order is given at a specific price with the understanding that the pit broker will attempt to fill your order three times in succession at the requested price. Hence, if you have an FOK order to sell at 4550, the broker who gets your order will offer at 4550 three times. If there is no fill, the broker will immediately cancel, or "kill," your order, and the kill will be reported back to you. The advantage of this order is that you will be able to place it at a specific price, and you will get very quick feedback as to whether it has been filled. And that's important!

Be aware, however, that not all exchanges or brokers accept FOK orders. Under certain market conditions such orders may be refused. Some brokers will become irritated if you use too many FOK orders that go unfilled, since it takes time and person power to place these orders. Discount brokers may be especially unhappy if you use too many FOK orders.

Finally, do not place your orders too far from the market, or they will not get filled. This will be even more aggravating for your broker. If you plan to use FOK orders, then please use orders that are very close to the current price. If you abuse these orders you will frustrate your broker and you will lose the respect of the order takers.

FOK orders are useful in virtually all situations where entry at the market should be avoided but where there is a need to establish or liquidate a position. Remember that using an FOK order does not guarantee a price fill, it merely guarantees that you will be filled at your price or better or not at all.

Stop Orders

Stop orders are placed either above or below the market. These orders are especially good for exiting positions when they go against you or for entering markets on breakouts. The problem with stop orders is that you will not necessarily be filled at your price in a fast market. Frequently many sharp and sudden moves in the currencies, T-bond futures, or S&P futures will result in considerable slippage of buy-and-sell stop orders. The best way to avoid this is to use a stop limit order, described below.

Stop Limit Orders

A stop limit order is a stop order with a price limit on it. The reason for using such an order is to allow more flexibility in obtaining a fill. Therefore, when you place a buy stop limit order at 6450 with a limit of 6465, this means that you will accept a fill within these limits inclusive. The good part of such an order is that it permits the floor broker more leeway in filling you and therefore improves the odds that you will be filled. Such an order protects you from too much slippage. Stop limit orders should be used more often by traders, although few traders actually use them.

Good-Til-Canceled Orders

A Good-Til-Canceled Order does exactly what its name suggests. It is an order which will remain in the market until canceled or filled. This order is also called an *open order*. Typically all open orders are canceled by your broker at the end of each calendar month and must be reinstated. In practice, day traders have no need for GTC or open orders, since their work is done at the end of each day.

One Cancels the Other (OCO)

This is an order qualifier. It allows a trader to have two orders entered simultaneously with the cancellation of one contingent upon the fulfillment of the other. In other words, when one of the orders is filled, the other will be canceled. This is a good way of bracketing markets for either of two possible outcomes. As in the case of several other orders noted previously, some exchanges do not accept such orders.

Using Orders to Your Advantage

Now that you've read about the different kinds of orders, here are some suggestions regarding their use. The purpose of learning how to use price orders to your advantage is obvious. Profitable day trading depends on making every penny and every point count. You must be consistent and frugal in everything you do. Here is a list of dos and don'ts with respect to orders:

- *Try to avoid using market orders* unless absolutely necessary. Market orders cost you ticks. If you lose a few ticks getting in and a few ticks getting out, then you have lost good money, often unnecessarily. There are many good alternatives to market orders. Some of them have been discussed above, some will be discussed below.

- *Don't use MOC orders.* They will cost you ticks. Ticks add up. A few ticks here, a few ticks there, pretty soon it adds up to real money. If you must use such an order then you are probably better off selling at the market several minutes before the close than in giving your broker an MOC order. As far as I'm concerned an MOC is, most often, a license to steal.

- *Use stop limit orders instead of stop orders.* In most cases you will be filled. If you are concerned about being filled, put a one- or two-tick limit on your order.

- *Fill-or-kill orders can be used to your advantage in several ways.* If you need to exit or enter a trade and you don't want to wait to find out if you've been filled then use an FOK order. You'll get quick feedback, and you'll probably save money. If you've never used such orders before, then get your feet wet.

- *Use FOK orders to test a market.* One good way to see how strong or weak a market may be is to use an FOK order. Here's what I mean. Let's say that June S&P futures are trading between 406.50 and 406.90. You had a buy signal at 406.50. Trading volume is light. Following the buy signal, prices moved quickly to 406.90, and you didn't want to chase the market. You are concerned that the signal might not work this time, because the market fell back quickly to the original breakout price of 406.50. You are hesitant to buy, therefore. What to do? Test the market by placing an FOK order to go long at 406.45 or 406.40, knowing that this is below the recent range of trades. Your order goes in and you watch the tape. It reads 406.55 when you enter your order. The ticks then go as follows: 406.55...406.50...406.55...406.50... 406.50...406.45B (your bid)...406.45. You are filled at your bid price. What does this mean about the character of the market? Most likely this indicates a market that is weak. You were filled at a low bid, and this means that there are willing sellers. This characterizes a weak market.

However, consider the same scenario with a different outcome. You enter your bid at 406.45 FOK. The tape reads 406.55 when you enter your order. The ticks then go as follows: 406.55...406.50...406.55... 406.50...406.50...406.55B...406.55...406.60...406.65...406.60...406.55... 406.60...406.65...406.70...406.75 and so on. The market never even comes close to your bid, and the order is returned killed. What does this mean? It indicates a market with good demand. It suggests that you had better get on board quickly. You may even want to use a market order to do so.

- *MIT orders are acceptable but not always efficient.* They are good for trading within a support/resistance channel, but they will cost you ticks.

- *OCO orders, where accepted, are very helpful.* They will help you bracket the market with different strategies and should be used wherever needed.

- *Specify first open only.* Some New York markets have staggered openings. In these markets each contract month is opened individually in chronological order, traded for a few minutes, and then closed so that another month may be opened. Once the process has been completed all months are opened again at the same time. The same procedure is used for closing. Should you need to get into one of these markets on the open, specify that you want your order good for the first open only. All too often the second opening price is distinctly different from the first open. This can cost you money.

- *Insist on prompt reporting of order fills.* It is absolutely necessary for you to know when you've been filled and when you've not been filled. You must be strict with your broker in demanding fills back as soon as possible. Do not accept excuses, particularly in currencies, T-bonds, S&P, and petroleum futures, where *flash fills* are easily given. A flash fill is one for which you may remain on hold as your order is hand-signaled to the pit. Although there will be some conditions in which delays are understandable, such delays are anathema to the day trader and must be avoided whenever and wherever possible.

- *Know which exchanges will accept certain orders.* The rules change from time to time and from one market condition to another. If you don't know the rules, find them out. The Chicago Mercantile and IMM will accept almost all orders almost all the time. The Chicago Board of Trade is a stickler for accepting only certain types of orders—it does not accept MITs. Some New York markets have restrictions as well. Orange juice is one of the most notorious markets, but then you probably don't want to and shouldn't day trade OJ.

- *Find out how your broker places your orders.* Does he or she call the floor? Are your orders put on a wire for execution? Does your broker need to call someone who will call someone else who will then call someone else? This all takes time. Day traders can't afford the time for such delays. Ask your broker for his or her procedures and deal only with those brokers who can get you the fastest fills. Anything else will cost you money no matter how low the commission rate. Don't be penny wise and pound foolish.

■ *Globex (24-hour) trading requires even more discretion in order placement.* Be very careful. Learn the rules and learn to deal with the lack of liquidity.

■ *If trading futures options, use price orders all the time.* A market order in options will frequently bring you shockingly bad results due to the poor liquidity. *Always* use price orders in futures options!

■ *Learn how to place orders.* Make sure your terminology is correct, make certain you mean what you say, and make sure you listen to the order as it is repeated back to you. You are liable for your orders. Errors will cost you.

■ *Don't beat around the bush.* When you place your orders, speak quickly, decisively, and clearly.

■ *Keep a written record of your orders.* Even if you trade only one market, once a day, keep a written record which includes the market, whether you bought or sold, the type of order, the quantity, the price you were filled at, your order number (as given to you by the order taker), and the time you placed the order. Don't fail to note all the above. It will save you a great deal of money in the long run.

■ *Report all errors immediately.* The longer you wait to report an error, the smaller the odds of having it rectified.

■ *Always, always, always, always check out at the end of the day, especially if you have traded a great deal.* By *check out* I mean make certain you have received all your fills and that you have closed out all your trades. Many brokerage firms will send you a preliminary run at the end of the day via modem. Print out the run and check it against your order sheet. Report all errors immediately!

■ *Check your order sheet before market closing to make certain you have taken the necessary steps to close out positions.* The more you trade and the larger your positions, the more important this will be.

These are just a few suggestions which will help you master the pragmatic end of day trading. Don't ever discount the importance of proper order placement and consistent procedures. The wrong order in the wrong market can cost you plenty. I know. I've made all these mistakes at one time or another, and I don't want you to have to repeat them. Learn it from me the easy way—don't learn it the hard way by losing money.

16

How Seasonality Influences Markets

A *seasonal price tendency* is the tendency of a market to move in a given direction at given times of the year. Seasonal price tendencies exert a significant influence in all markets. Although some markets are more prone to react on a seasonal basis, I know no markets which are totally immune from such responses. The day trader who is familiar with seasonality can use it to his or her advantage. Seasonal influences cause markets to move in a given direction a large majority of the time during certain weeks, months, and even calendar dates. Art Merrill, in his classic book, *The Behavior of Prices on Wall Street* (Analysis Press, Chappaqua, New York), demonstrated this phenomenon statistically. He proved definitively that the Dow Jones Industrial Average was prone to close higher the day before certain holidays a large percentage of the time. His statistical base dated back over 100 years, and thus the odds that his findings were random events or chance results were less than 1 in 10,000.

Defining Key Seasonal Dates

My work with futures markets has revealed essentially similar results to those of Merrill, and these results may be used to the distinct advantage of the day trader. Specifically, I am referring to the use of what I have termed *key seasonal dates*. A key seasonal date is a date on which a given market has shown a strong tendency to close higher or lower a large percentage of the time. There are many such dates throughout the year, but not all are reliable. The larger the number of cases we have observed, the more reliable the key date. As an example, consider the chart in Figure 16-1. It shows the daily seasonal tendency for March copper futures. As you can see, I've marked certain dates with arrows up and down. The numbers inside the squares show date, and above

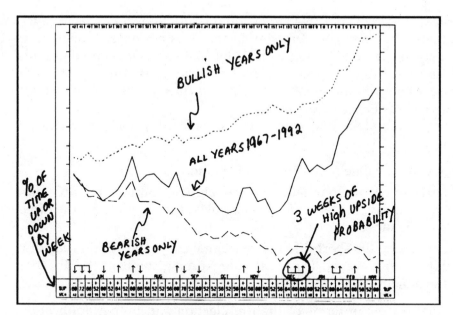

Figure 16-1. Seasonal tendency in March copper futures.

these numbers appears the percentage of time the given market has closed up or down on this day. Naturally if the market is closed on a given date then the reading cannot be used for trading this year.

The solid line plot shows the seasonal tendency. Arrows up and arrows down mark dates which have shown a strong percentage of time up or down. By this I mean that the arrows up show dates on which the closing price has been higher a large percentage of the time whereas arrows down show markets which closed lower on this date a large percentage of the time. The exact percentage appears in the box above the date. Although there are many arrows up and down, this does not guarantee that the market will move in its anticipated direction this year.

How to Use the Key Seasonal Date Tendencies

The key date tendencies should serve as a guide or a preselection factor. Look for the following characteristics:

1. Percentage of time up close 75 percent of the time or more
2. Percentage of time down close 75 percent of the time or more
3. Fairly large magnitude of move as shown on the solid line plot

Figures 16-2, 16-3, and 16-4 show you my selections for dates in several markets. The process is very simple and does not require much judgment as you can see. But this is just the first step. Once the dates and markets have been selected, you will need to apply timing. This will increase your odds for success. It will help filter out trades which will not move in the expected direction.

Here are the steps and rules I use in selecting seasonal dates for trading:

1. Pick your key date trades for the next date.
2. For trades on the long side use buy signals confirming entry only during the day; however, *do not buy* unless timing confirms the direction of the move.
3. For trades on the short side use sell signal confirming entry only during the day; however, *do not sell* unless timing confirms the direction of the move.

It's that simple in terms of the preselection and timing application. There are many timing signals you can use with the seasonals. Figures 16-5, 16-6, and 16-7 illustrate my approach using timing and key date seasonals.

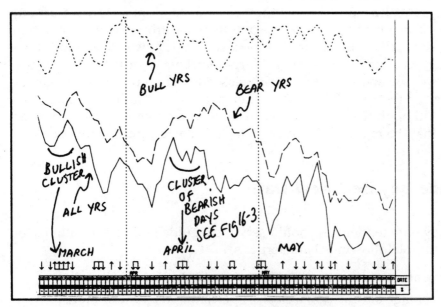

Figure 16-2. Finding daily seasonal trades in Swiss franc futures.

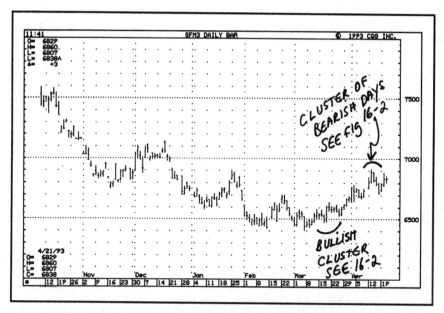

Figure 16-3. Finding daily seasonal trades in Swiss franc futures.

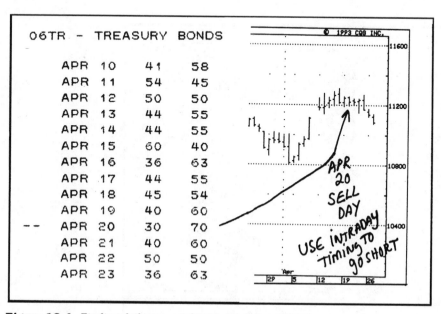

Figure 16-4. Finding daily seasonal trades in T-bond futures.

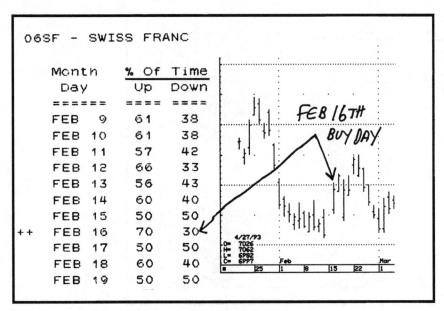

Figure 16-5. Key dates and timing.

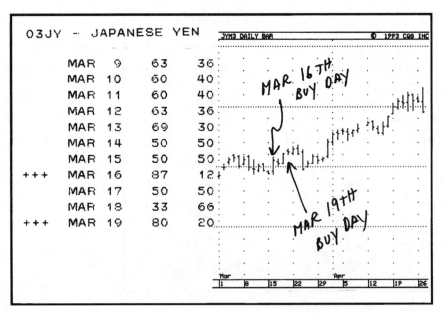

Figure 16-6. Key dates and timing.

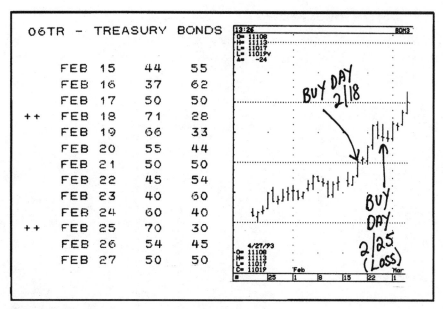

Figure 16-7. Key dates and timing.

Daily Seasonal Tendencies

Many markets exhibit strong seasonality on a daily basis. Although it could be argued statistically that a lengthier data history is needed for some of the daily seasonals, the fact is that seasonals do exist and that their reliability has been aptly demonstrated and validated by Art Merrill in his classic book, *The Behavior of Prices on Wall Street.*

Since daily seasonals work best in the most active markets where the largest intraday moves are likely, I urge you to restrict your trading to these markets. In order to assist you in this venture, I am providing you below with my latest daily seasonal listings in S&P, Swiss franc, and T-bond futures in Figures 16-8, 16-9, and 16-10. Note that these listings will change each year as more data are available. Should you wish to acquire up-to-date listings, please contact my office (MBH Commodity Advisors, Inc., P.O. Box 353, Winnetka, Ill. 60093). Please read the instructions in Figure 16-8 for interpreting the lists.

Daily Seasonals S&P Futures

Handwritten annotations: PROBABILITY OF MOVE · DATE · LOOK FOR 62% OR HIGHER · AVERAGE SIZE OF MOVE

	Month Day	% Of Time Up	% Of Time Down	Average % Up	Average % Down	Years in Sample Up	Years in Sample Down	Years in Sample Unch.	Years in Sample Total
++	AUG 9	75	25	.26	-.08	6	2	0	8
	AUG 10	50	50	.38	-.06	4	4	0	8
++	AUG 11	71	28	.35	-.10	5	2	0	7
++	AUG 12	75	25	.35	-.10	6	2	0	8
+	AUG 13	62	37	.38	-.07	5	3	0	8
++	AUG 14	75	25	.40	-.02	6	2	0	8
+++	AUG 15	87	12	.26	-.04	7	1	0	8
+	AUG 16	62	37	.29	-.08	5	3	0	8
	AUG 17	50	50	.38	-.06	4	4	0	8
++	AUG 18	71	28	.36	-.06	5	2	0	7
+++	AUG 19	85	14	.34	-.09	6	1	0	7
	AUG 20	50	50	.46	-.05	4	4	0	8
++	AUG 21	75	25	.40	-.11	6	2	0	8
+	AUG 22	62	37	.36	-.08	5	3	0	8
	AUG 23	50	50	.37	-.09	4	4	0	8
+	AUG 24	62	37	.31	-.13	5	3	0	8
++	AUG 25	71	28	.37	-.06	5	2	0	7
++	AUG 26	75	25	.37	-.05	6	2	0	8
	AUG 27	50	50	.51	-.07	4	4	0	8
+	AUG 28	62	37	.51	-.08	5	3	0	8
++	AUG 29	75	25	.33	-.07	6	2	0	8
+	AUG 30	62	37	.32	-.07	5	3	0	8
+	AUG 31	62	37	.31	-.08	5	3	0	8
	SEP 1	50	50	.52	-.03	3	3	0	6
+++	SEP 2	83	16	.29	-.04	5	1	0	6
+++	SEP 3	83	16	.39	-.04	5	1	0	6
	SEP 4	57	42	.47	-.08	4	3	0	7
+	SEP 5	66	33	.41	-.08	4	2	0	6
++	SEP 6	71	28	.32	-.10	5	2	0	7
+	SEP 7	66	33	.21	-.10	4	2	0	6
+++	SEP 8	85	14	.31	-.08	6	1	0	7
+++	SEP 9	87	12	.31	-.06	7	1	0	8
+	SEP 10	62	37	.36	-.08	5	3	0	8
+	SEP 11	62	37	.43	-.08	5	3	0	8
++	SEP 12	75	25	.27	-.10	6	2	0	8
+++	SEP 13	87	12	.21	-.20	7	1	0	8
+++	SEP 14	87	12	.23	-.22	7	1	0	8
+++	SEP 15	85	14	.28	-.03	6	1	0	7

Handwritten annotations: GOOD ONES TO TRADE (AUG 11) · BEST TRADES (AUG 15) · FAIR (AUG 22) · 2 IN A ROW IS GOOD (SEP 6) · GREAT! (SEP 11) · 4 IN A ROW (SEP 12)

Figure 16-8. Daily seasonals, S&P futures.

	Month Day	% Of Time Up	Down	--- Average % --- Up	Down	Years in Sample Up	Down	Unch	Total
+++	SEP 16	87	12	.28	-.03	7	1	0	8
++	SEP 17	75	25	.26	-.12	6	2	0	8
+++	SEP 18	87	12	.29	-.20	7	1	0	8
++	SEP 19	75	25	.27	-.12	6	2	0	8
++	SEP 20	75	25	.27	-.14	6	2	0	8
+	SEP 21	62	37	.32	-.10	5	3	0	8
+++	SEP 22	85	14	.30	-.05	6	1	0	7
+++	SEP 23	87	12	.30	-.05	7	1	0	8
+	SEP 24	62	37	.34	-.14	5	3	0	8
+	SEP 25	62	37	.40	-.14	5	3	0	8
++	SEP 26	75	25	.27	-.17	6	2	0	8
+++	SEP 27	87	12	.22	-.39	7	1	0	8
+	SEP 28	62	37	.33	-.14	5	3	0	8
+++	SEP 29	85	14	.30	-.05	6	1	0	7
+++	SEP 30	87	12	.29	-.04	7	1	0	8
+	OCT 1	62	37	.34	-.11	5	3	0	8
+	OCT 2	62	37	.43	-.14	5	3	0	8
++	OCT 3	75	25	.28	-.17	6	2	0	8
++	OCT 4	75	25	.26	-.16	6	2	0	8
+	OCT 5	62	37	.35	-.16	5	3	0	8
+++	OCT 6	85	14	.33	-.16	6	1	0	7
+++	OCT 7	87	12	.30	-.19	7	1	0	8
+	OCT 8	62	37	.33	-.15	5	3	0	8
+	OCT 9	62	37	.40	-.21	5	3	0	8
++	OCT 10	75	25	.31	-.23	6	2	0	8
++	OCT 11	75	25	.30	-.25	6	2	0	8
+	OCT 12	62	37	.35	-.20	5	3	0	8
+++	OCT 13	85	14	.29	-.13	6	1	0	7
+++	OCT 14	87	12	.30	-.14	7	1	0	8
+	OCT 15	62	37	.33	-.17	5	3	0	8
+	OCT 16	62	37	.35	-.19	5	3	0	8
++	OCT 17	75	25	.30	-.23	6	2	0	8
+++	OCT 18	87	12	.26	-.34	7	1	0	8
	OCT 19	50	50	.26	-.20	4	4	0	8
++	OCT 20	71	28	.26	-.18	5	2	0	7
+++	OCT 21	87	12	.25	-.07	7	1	0	8
	OCT 22	50	50	.27	-.09	4	4	0	8
	OCT 23	50	50	.34	-.10	4	4	0	8

Figure 16-8. Daily seasonals, S&P futures. (*Continued*)

	Month Day	% Of Time		--- Average % ---		----- Years in Sample -----			
		Up	Down	Up	Down	Up	Down	Unch	Total
	======	====	====	========	========	=====	=====	=====	=====
++	OCT 24	75	25	.29	-.13	6	2	0	8
++	OCT 25	75	25	.28	-.17	6	2	0	8
	OCT 26	50	50	.24	-.17	4	4	0	8
++	OCT 27	71	28	.22	-.10	5	2	0	7
++	OCT 28	75	25	.25	-.08	6	2	0	8
+	OCT 29	62	37	.23	-.15	5	3	0	8
+	OCT 30	62	37	.30	-.14	5	3	0	8
++	OCT 31	75	25	.30	-.19	6	2	0	8
++	NOV 1	75	25	.29	-.17	6	2	0	8
+	NOV 2	62	37	.22	-.10	5	3	0	8
+++	NOV 3	85	14	.22	-.03	6	1	0	7
+++	NOV 4	87	12	.25	-.07	7	1	0	8
+	NOV 5	62	37	.28	-.11	5	3	0	8
++	NOV 6	75	25	.23	-.18	6	2	0	8
++	NOV 7	75	25	.29	-.18	6	2	0	8
++	NOV 8	75	25	.29	-.17	6	2	0	8
+	NOV 9	62	37	.19	-.11	5	3	0	8
++	NOV 10	71	28	.24	-.05	5	2	0	7
++	NOV 11	75	25	.29	-.01	6	2	0	8
++	NOV 12	75	25	.24	-.12	6	2	0	8
++	NOV 13	75	25	.26	-.14	6	2	0	8
++	NOV 14	75	25	.31	-.12	6	2	0	8
++	NOV 15	75	25	.27	-.14	6	2	0	8
+	NOV 16	62	37	.17	-.10	5	3	0	8
++	NOV 17	71	28	.21	-.03	5	2	0	7
+++	NOV 18	100	0	.19	.00	8	0	0	8
+	NOV 19	62	37	.23	-.11	5	3	0	8
+	NOV 20	62	37	.27	-.11	5	3	0	8
++	NOV 21	75	25	.28	-.15	6	2	0	8
+++	NOV 22	100	0	.26	.00	6	0	0	6
	NOV 23	57	42	.12	-.10	4	3	0	7
+++	NOV 24	100	0	.18	.00	5	0	0	5
+++	NOV 25	83	16	.23	.00	5	1	0	6
+	NOV 26	66	33	.31	-.14	4	2	0	6
	NOV 27	57	42	.31	-.11	4	3	0	7
+	NOV 28	66	33	.25	-.14	4	2	0	6
++	NOV 29	75	25	.27	-.16	6	2	0	8
+	NOV 30	62	37	.21	-.13	5	3	0	8

Figure 16-8. Daily seasonals, S&P futures. (*Continued*)

	Month Day	% Of Time		--- Average % ---		----- Years in Sample -----			
		Up	Down	Up	Down	Up	Down	Unch	Total
	AUG 9	50	50	.04	-.04	5	5	0	10
--	AUG 10	27	72	.05	-.05	3	8	0	11
-	AUG 11	40	60	.08	-.06	4	6	0	10
	AUG 12	50	50	.06	-.06	5	5	0	10
	AUG 13	45	54	.06	-.06	5	6	0	11
	AUG 14	41	50	.07	-.07	5	6	1	12
	AUG 15	36	54	.08	-.05	4	6	1	11
	AUG 16	40	50	.05	-.04	4	5	1	10
-	AUG 17	27	63	.06	-.05	3	7	1	11
-	AUG 18	40	60	.09	-.06	4	6	0	10
	AUG 19	44	55	.08	-.07	4	5	0	9
	AUG 20	45	54	.08	-.06	5	6	0	11
	AUG 21	41	58	.08	-.06	5	7	0	12
-	AUG 22	36	63	.09	-.04	4	7	0	11
-	AUG 23	40	60	.06	-.04	4	6	0	10
--	AUG 24	27	72	.06	-.05	3	8	0	11
-	AUG 25	40	60	.09	-.06	4	6	0	10
	AUG 26	50	50	.07	-.07	5	5	0	10
	AUG 27	45	54	.07	-.08	5	6	0	11
	AUG 28	41	58	.08	-.07	5	7	0	12
-	AUG 29	36	63	.10	-.05	4	7	0	11
-	AUG 30	40	60	.06	-.04	4	6	0	10
-	AUG 31	36	63	.04	-.06	4	7	0	11
	SEP 1	50	50	.04	-.08	4	4	0	8
	SEP 2	50	50	.07	-.10	4	4	0	8
+	SEP 3	62	37	.07	-.12	5	3	0	8
-	SEP 4	40	60	.07	-.08	4	6	0	10
	SEP 5	44	55	.08	-.05	4	5	0	9
	SEP 6	44	55	.05	-.04	4	5	0	9
-	SEP 7	37	62	.06	-.04	3	5	0	8
	SEP 8	50	50	.07	-.09	5	5	0	10
+	SEP 9	60	40	.06	-.10	6	4	0	10
	SEP 10	45	54	.06	-.08	5	6	0	11
	SEP 11	41	58	.07	-.07	5	7	0	12
	SEP 12	45	54	.07	-.05	5	6	0	11
	SEP 13	50	50	.05	-.04	5	5	0	10
-	SEP 14	36	63	.06	-.06	4	7	0	11
	SEP 15	50	50	.07	-.09	5	5	0	10

Figure 16-9. Daily seasonals, T-bond futures.

	Month Day	% Of Time Up	% Of Time Down	--- Average % --- Up	Down	----- Years in Sample ----- Up	Down	Unch	Total
+	SEP 16	60	40	.06	-.10	6	4	0	10
	SEP 17	45	54	.06	-.08	5	6	0	11
	SEP 18	41	58	.07	-.07	5	7	0	12
	SEP 19	54	45	.05	-.06	6	5	0	11
+	SEP 20	60	40	.05	-.05	6	4	0	10
-	SEP 21	36	63	.06	-.06	4	7	0	11
	SEP 22	45	54	.07	-.08	5	6	0	11
	SEP 23	54	45	.06	-.09	6	5	0	11
	SEP 24	45	54	.07	-.09	5	6	0	11
	SEP 25	41	58	.07	-.09	5	7	0	12
	SEP 26	41	58	.07	-.05	5	7	0	12
	SEP 27	54	45	.05	-.04	6	5	0	11
-	SEP 28	33	66	.06	-.06	4	8	0	12
	SEP 29	45	54	.07	-.09	5	6	0	11
	SEP 30	54	45	.07	-.09	6	5	0	11
	OCT 1	45	54	.08	-.09	5	6	0	11
	OCT 2	41	58	.08	-.08	5	7	0	12
	OCT 3	41	58	.08	-.05	5	7	0	12
	OCT 4	45	54	.06	-.04	5	6	0	11
-	OCT 5	33	66	.06	-.06	4	8	0	12
	OCT 6	45	54	.08	-.08	5	6	0	11
	OCT 7	54	45	.07	-.08	6	5	0	11
	OCT 8	45	54	.08	-.09	5	6	0	11
	OCT 9	41	58	.07	-.08	5	7	0	12
	OCT 10	41	58	.08	-.05	5	7	0	12
	OCT 11	45	54	.08	-.05	5	6	0	11
-	OCT 12	33	66	.08	-.07	4	8	0	12
	OCT 13	45	54	.09	-.08	5	6	0	11
	OCT 14	54	45	.07	-.09	6	5	0	11
	OCT 15	45	54	.08	-.09	5	6	0	11
	OCT 16	41	58	.07	-.09	5	7	0	12
	OCT 17	50	50	.06	-.06	6	6	0	12
	OCT 18	54	45	.07	-.05	6	5	0	11
	OCT 19	41	58	.07	-.08	5	7	0	12
	OCT 20	45	54	.08	-.09	5	6	0	11
	OCT 21	54	45	.07	-.09	6	5	0	11
	OCT 22	54	45	.07	-.11	6	5	0	11
	OCT 23	50	50	.07	-.10	6	6	0	12

Figure 16-9. Daily seasonals, T-bond futures. (*Continued*)

	Month Day	% Of Time		--- Average % ---		----- Years in Sample -----			
		Up	Down	Up	Down	Up	Down	Unch	Total
	OCT 24	50	50	.07	-.07	6	6	0	12
	OCT 25	54	45	.07	-.06	6	5	0	11
	OCT 26	41	58	.06	-.08	5	7	0	12
	OCT 27	45	54	.09	-.09	5	6	0	11
	OCT 28	54	45	.07	-.09	6	5	0	11
	OCT 29	54	45	.07	-.11	6	5	0	11
	OCT 30	50	50	.08	-.10	6	6	0	12
	OCT 31	50	50	.08	-.08	6	6	0	12
	NOV 1	54	45	.08	-.06	6	5	0	11
-	NOV 2	36	63	.05	-.08	4	7	0	11
	NOV 3	45	54	.10	-.08	5	6	0	11
+	NOV 4	60	40	.09	-.06	6	4	0	10
	NOV 5	54	45	.08	-.10	6	5	0	11
	NOV 6	41	58	.09	-.08	5	7	0	12
	NOV 7	54	45	.08	-.08	6	5	0	11
	NOV 8	54	45	.08	-.06	6	5	0	11
-	NOV 9	33	66	.08	-.06	4	8	0	12
	NOV 10	45	54	.09	-.08	5	6	0	11
	NOV 11	54	45	.08	-.07	6	5	0	11
	NOV 12	54	45	.08	-.09	6	5	0	11
	NOV 13	50	50	.08	-.08	6	6	0	12
	NOV 14	50	50	.08	-.07	6	6	0	12
	NOV 15	54	45	.08	-.05	6	5	0	11
	NOV 16	41	58	.07	-.06	5	7	0	12
	NOV 17	45	54	.09	-.07	5	6	0	11
	NOV 18	54	45	.09	-.07	6	5	0	11
	NOV 19	54	45	.09	-.09	6	5	0	11
	NOV 20	50	50	.09	-.08	6	6	0	12
	NOV 21	50	50	.09	-.07	6	6	0	12
+	NOV 22	62	37	.09	-.04	5	3	0	8
-	NOV 23	40	60	.06	-.06	4	6	0	10
	NOV 24	50	50	.12	-.09	4	4	0	8
	NOV 25	50	50	.07	-.07	5	5	0	10
+	NOV 26	62	37	.10	-.09	5	3	0	8
	NOV 27	50	50	.07	-.06	5	5	0	10
-	NOV 28	40	60	.09	-.07	4	6	0	10
	NOV 29	54	45	.08	-.05	6	5	0	11
	NOV 30	41	58	.07	-.05	5	7	0	12

Figure 16-9. Daily seasonals, T-bond futures. (*Continued*)

Month Day	% Of Time		--- Average % ---		----- Years in Sample -----			
	Up	Down	Up	Down	Up	Down	Unch	Total
- AUG 9	33	66	.06	-.08	4	8	0	12
- AUG 10	38	61	.06	-.08	5	8	0	13
- AUG 11	38	61	.06	-.08	5	8	0	13
- AUG 12	38	61	.05	-.09	5	8	0	13
AUG 13	46	53	.07	-.08	6	7	0	13
AUG 14	46	53	.08	-.08	6	7	0	13
- AUG 15	30	69	.10	-.07	4	9	0	13
- AUG 16	33	66	.08	-.08	4	8	0	12
- AUG 17	38	61	.08	-.08	5	8	0	13
- AUG 18	38	61	.07	-.08	5	8	0	13
- AUG 19	33	66	.05	-.09	4	8	0	12
AUG 20	46	53	.08	-.08	6	7	0	13
AUG 21	46	53	.09	-.07	6	7	0	13
- AUG 22	30	69	.10	-.07	4	9	0	13
AUG 23	41	58	.06	-.09	5	7	0	12
AUG 24	46	53	.07	-.09	6	7	0	13
AUG 25	46	53	.06	-.09	6	7	0	13
AUG 26	46	53	.06	-.10	6	7	0	13
AUG 27	46	53	.08	-.08	6	7	0	13
AUG 28	46	53	.09	-.07	6	7	0	13
- AUG 29	38	61	.08	-.08	5	8	0	13
AUG 30	41	58	.06	-.10	5	7	0	12
AUG 31	46	53	.07	-.10	6	7	0	13
SEP 1	50	50	.06	-.11	5	5	0	10
SEP 2	45	54	.06	-.09	5	6	0	11
SEP 3	50	50	.07	-.09	5	5	0	10
SEP 4	45	54	.09	-.08	5	6	0	11
- SEP 5	40	60	.09	-.07	4	6	0	10
- SEP 6	40	60	.07	-.09	4	6	0	10
- SEP 7	40	60	.06	-.09	4	6	0	10
SEP 8	46	53	.07	-.09	6	7	0	13
SEP 9	46	53	.05	-.09	6	7	0	13
SEP 10	46	53	.07	-.08	6	7	0	13
SEP 11	46	53	.08	-.07	6	7	0	13
- SEP 12	38	61	.07	-.08	5	8	0	13
SEP 13	41	58	.06	-.09	5	7	0	12
SEP 14	46	53	.07	-.10	6	7	0	13
SEP 15	46	53	.06	-.09	6	7	0	13

Figure 16-10. Daily seasonals, Swiss franc futures.

Month	% Of Time		--- Average % ---		----- Years in Sample ----			
Day	Up	Down	Up	Down	Up	Down	Unch	Tota
======	====	====	========	========	======	======	======	=====
SEP 16	46	53	.05	-.09	6	7	0	13
SEP 17	46	53	.08	-.07	6	7	0	13
SEP 18	46	53	.09	-.07	6	7	0	13
— SEP 19	38	61	.08	-.08	5	8	0	13
SEP 20	41	58	.06	-.09	5	7	0	12
SEP 21	46	53	.07	-.09	6	7	0	13
SEP 22	46	53	.07	-.09	6	7	0	13
SEP 23	46	53	.05	-.09	6	7	0	13
SEP 24	46	53	.08	-.07	6	7	0	13
SEP 25	46	53	.10	-.07	6	7	0	13
— SEP 26	38	61	.09	-.08	5	8	0	13
SEP 27	41	58	.08	-.09	5	7	0	12
SEP 28	46	53	.08	-.09	6	7	0	13
SEP 29	46	53	.08	-.09	6	7	0	13
SEP 30	46	53	.06	-.09	6	7	0	13
OCT 1	46	53	.09	-.07	6	7	0	13
OCT 2	46	53	.10	-.06	6	7	0	13
— OCT 3	38	61	.09	-.07	5	8	0	13
OCT 4	41	58	.07	-.09	5	7	0	12
OCT 5	46	53	.08	-.08	6	7	0	13
OCT 6	46	53	.07	-.08	6	7	0	13
OCT 7	46	53	.06	-.09	6	7	0	13
OCT 8	46	53	.08	-.07	6	7	0	13
OCT 9	46	53	.10	-.06	6	7	0	13
— OCT 10	38	61	.09	-.08	5	8	0	13
OCT 11	41	58	.08	-.09	5	7	0	12
OCT 12	46	53	.08	-.09	6	7	0	13
OCT 13	46	53	.07	-.08	6	7	0	13
OCT 14	46	53	.06	-.08	6	7	0	13
OCT 15	46	53	08	-.08	6	7	0	13
OCT 16	46	53	.10	-.07	6	7	0	13
— OCT 17	38	61	.10	-.08	5	8	0	13
OCT 18	41	58	.08	-.09	5	7	0	12
OCT 19	46	53	.08	-.09	6	7	0	13
OCT 20	46	53	.07	-.08	6	7	0	13
OCT 21	46	53	.06	-.09	6	7	0	13
OCT 22	46	53	.08	-.08	6	7	0	13
OCT 23	46	53	.10	-.07	6	7	0	13

Figure 16-10. Daily seasonals, Swiss franc futures. (*Continued*)

Month Day	% Of Time Up	% Of Time Down	--- Average % --- Up	--- Average % --- Down	----- Years in Sample ----- Up	----- Years in Sample ----- Down	----- Years in Sample ----- Unch	----- Years in Sample ----- Total
- OCT 24	38	61	.09	-.08	5	8	0	13
OCT 25	41	58	.08	-.09	5	7	0	12
OCT 26	46	53	.08	-.09	6	7	0	13
OCT 27	46	53	.07	-.08	6	7	0	13
OCT 28	46	53	.06	-.09	6	7	0	13
OCT 29	46	53	.08	-.08	6	7	0	13
OCT 30	46	53	.10	-.07	6	7	0	13
- OCT 31	38	61	.10	-.08	5	8	0	13
NOV 1	41	58	.08	-.09	5	7	0	12
NOV 2	41	58	.09	-.08	5	7	0	12
NOV 3	46	53	.06	-.08	6	7	0	13
NOV 4	50	50	.06	-.09	6	6	0	12
NOV 5	46	53	.08	-.07	6	7	0	13
NOV 6	46	53	.09	-.06	6	7	0	13
- NOV 7	33	66	.09	-.07	4	8	0	12
NOV 8	41	58	.08	-.09	5	7	0	12
NOV 9	46	53	.08	-.08	6	7	0	13
NOV 10	46	53	.06	-.08	6	7	0	13
NOV 11	46	53	.06	-.08	6	7	0	13
NOV 12	46	53	.08	-.07	6	7	0	13
NOV 13	46	53	.09	-.06	6	7	0	13
- NOV 14	38	61	.09	-.07	5	8	0	13
NOV 15	41	58	.07	-.09	5	7	0	12
NOV 16	46	53	.07	-.08	6	7	0	13
NOV 17	46	53	.05	-.08	6	7	0	13
NOV 18	46	53	.06	-.08	6	7	0	13
NOV 19	46	53	.08	-.07	6	7	0	13
NOV 20	46	53	.09	-.06	6	7	0	13
- NOV 21	38	61	.08	-.07	5	8	0	13
NOV 22	44	55	.05	-.09	4	5	0	9
NOV 23	45	54	.07	-.09	5	6	0	11
NOV 24	44	55	.06	-.07	4	5	0	9
NOV 25	50	50	.07	-.07	5	5	0	10
- NOV 26	40	60	.09	-.08	4	6	0	10
NOV 27	50	50	.09	-.06	5	5	0	10
- NOV 28	36	63	.09	-.07	4	7	0	11
NOV 29	41	58	.07	-.08	5	7	0	12
NOV 30	46	53	.07	-.07	6	7	0	13

Figure 16-10. Daily seasonals, Swiss franc futures. (*Continued*)

17
Intraday Spread Trading

The futures spread is perhaps the least used and least understood vehicle in the world of futures trading. To most traders the idea of spreading a market is totally foreign. Can you imagine their surprise when I suggest trading spreads in the day time frame? Whereas many traders consider spreads to be an intermediate- to longer-term vehicle, I feel that some spreads can also provide day-trading opportunities. Provided you select the right spreads, you can use many of the technical tools I've described in this book as entry and exit methods.

As you know, a *futures spread* involves buying one contract and selling another. You are long and short at the same time. The contracts may be in the same markets or in different markets. In other words, you can be long June cattle and short October cattle which would constitute an intracommodity spread. You can buy July wheat and sell July corn. This is an intercommodity spread. Typically intercommodity spreads are better vehicles for day traders, since these spreads tend to exhibit more of the characteristics which are prerequisites to successful spread day trading.

Preselection: The Key to Profitable Spread Day Trading

The key to profitable trading spread is the preselection process. In other words, you need to select spreads for day trading which meet the following criteria:

1. *They must be volatile.* In other words, they must be spreads which tend to show sufficient price movement during the day to make them viable trading vehicles.
2. *They must have a sufficiently high tick value.* High tick value makes spreads worthwhile from the day-trading perspective.

163

3. *They must be sufficiently liquid.* Liquidity permits entry and exit without difficulty.

With these factors in mind I will now outline the processes and methods for day-trading spreads.

Methods of Spread Day Trading

Support and Resistance Levels. The most specific and basic method of day-trading spreads is to determine support and resistance levels at the end of the trading day and to use these levels as entry and exit points the next day. The chart shown in Figure 17-1 illustrates some simple support and resistance buy-and-sell points (i.e., by buy and sell I mean entry and exit points for the spread) using traditional support and resistance lines. This is, as you can easily see, a very simple and effective method for day-trading spreads.

Just remember that if you are day trading a spread then you must be in and out of the spread the same day. Do not carry the spread overnight, since this would, as you know, negate the entire purpose of day trading. Since the spreads you will be day trading are selected for their volatility, I urge you to avoid carrying them overnight in order to circumvent any nasty surprises the next day.

Thirty-Minute Timing with Stochastics. Now consider the same chart as shown in Figure 17-1 but with the addition of a 9-period slow stochastic indicator using SP and traditional stochastic timing signals as described in Chapter 5. Examine Figures 17-2 and 17-3. Please carefully study my notations. As you can see, stochastic timing methods for spread entry and exit have considerable potential provided there is sufficient movement in the spread to allow for intraday trading.

Spread Timing with RSI. Yet another method of timing intraday spread entry and exit is by using either a 14- or a 9-period RSI. Several methods of application are illustrated in Figures 17-4 through 17-7. Here is a synopsis of the methods:

- *RSI crossovers from below 50 and above 50.* This is a simple method. When RSI is 50 or over you will want to be bull spread (i.e., long front month and short back month). When RSI crosses from above 50 to below 50, you will want to be bear spread. If the crossover occurs during the day with sufficient time left for a trade, then you can initiate a position and/or reverse a previous position. Be out by the end of the

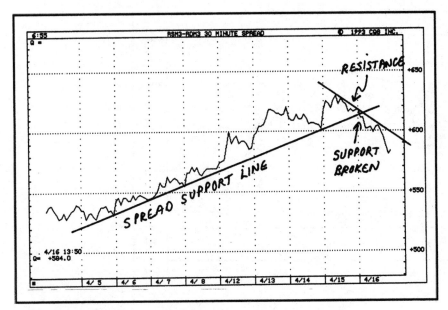

Figure 17-1. Support and resistance points: Intraday spread chart.

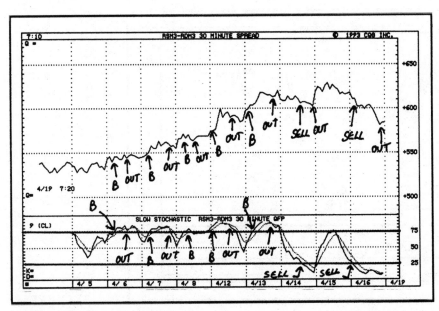

Figure 17-2. Intraday spread chart with stochastics and stochastic pop technique—entry and exit signals.

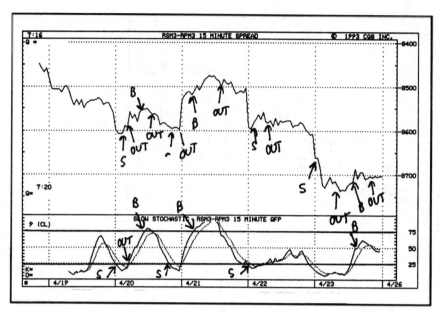

Figure 17-3. Intraday spread chart with stochastics and stochastic pop technique—entry and exit signals.

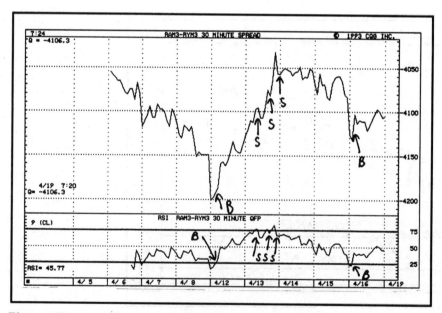

Figure 17-4. Intraday spread chart: RSI entry and exit signals.

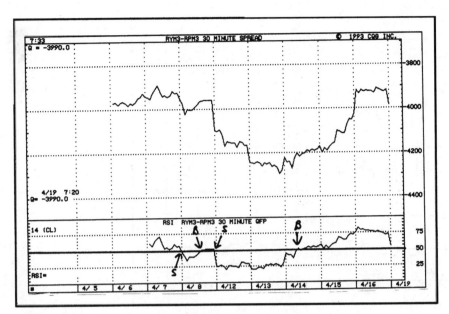

Figure 17-5. Intraday spread chart: RSI entry and exit signals.

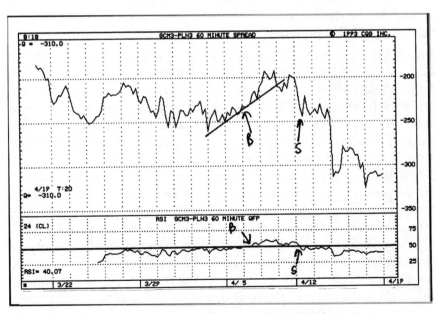

Figure 17-6. Intraday spread chart: RSI entry and exit signals.

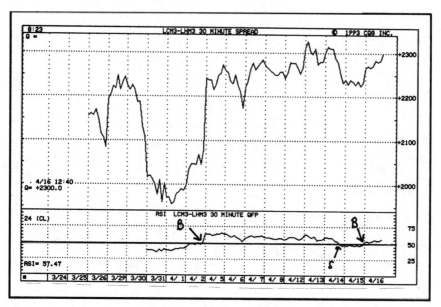

Figure 17-7. Intraday spread chart: RSI entry and exit signals.

day. The next day you can establish a new position in the spread consistent with the RSI reading and be out by the end of the day or reverse on a reversing signal. At times there will be several oscillations above and below the 50 percent RSI line. If this occurs too frequently, then use a longer RSI period (i.e., 18 or 24 as opposed to 9 or 14).

- *RSI crossovers from below 25 and above 75.* This is also a very simple method. When RSI is 75 or over you will be bull spread (i.e., long front month and short back month) from a previous buy entry. When RSI crosses from above 75 to below 75, you will want to be bear spread. If the crossover occurs during the day with sufficient time left for a trade, then you can initiate a position and/or reverse a previous position. Be out by the end of the day. The next day you can establish a new position in the spread consistent with the RSI reading and be out by the end of the day or reverse on a reversing signal. At times there will be several oscillations above and below the 50 percent RSI line. If this occurs too frequently, then use a longer RSI period (i.e., 18 or 24 as opposed to 9 or 14). If RSI is 25 or lower you will already be bear spread from a previous sell signal. If RSI then goes above 25, you will reverse positions and exit at the end of the day or on a reversing signal. At the beginning of the next day enter the spread again consistent with the RSI reading.

- *RSI first derivative crossovers.* This method is very specific and does not differ from the previously discussed RSI first moving average (MA) derivative method already discussed. The rules of application are simple. If RSI is below its MA derivative, then you will be bear spread. If RSI is above its first MA derivative, you will be bull spread. Exit at the end of the day or reverse during the day if there is a crossover signal. You can reinstate position the next day on or near the open consistent with the last signal.

What You Can Realistically Expect

Over the years I have developed both a strong liking as well as a strong respect for spreads and those who trade them well. Spreads can offer more conservative opportunities and higher probability of success. But to benefit from intraday spread trading, you will need to choose volatile spreads. Many of these are cross currency spreads, but there are times during which grain and livestock markets, cotton, interest rate, and inter-precious-metals spreads can be traded very effectively. You will need to remain aware of which spreads are sufficiently volatile and liquid for day trading. Finally, it is always best to use price orders for spreads, since market orders can prove very costly both on entry as well as on exit. As long as you remain aware of the risks, volatility, and liquidity of the spreads you are trading, then you can do very well trading spreads on an intraday basis.

18
The Consecutive Closes System

Yet another method of finding profitable day trades is what I call the *consecutive closes system*. The approach is simple. As the name indicates, this method generates buy and sell signals based on the number of consecutive higher or lower *closes*. Although markets post true closing prices at the end of each trading session, this does not, in fact, occur on an intraday basis. We simply refer to the last price of each 5-minute time segment as the *5-minute closing price*. In actuality, it is not a closing price but merely the price at the end of each 5 minutes. A 30-minute closing price would be the closing price at the end of each 30-minute time segment. While this is truly a simple concept, it never ceases to amaze me how many traders who are otherwise knowledgeable and intelligent fail to grasp the idea. Please make sure that you do before reading on.

Definitions and Signals

The consecutive closes system (CC) is based on a simple but profitable and sensible concept: Once a trend has established itself, it is best to go with that trend until and unless it changes. The problem is, as always, twofold. First, you need to identify the trend, and, second, you need to know when to get aboard the trend. The CC system achieves these goals as follows:

1. A buy signal and an up trend are defined when the market has made a given number of *up* closes in a row. Therefore, if we are using a signal which consists of five consecutive up closes in a row, we are using a 5CCU buy signal (5 consecutive closes up).

2. A sell signal and a down trend are defined when the market has made given number of *down* closes in a row. Therefore, if we are

170

using a signal which consists of five consecutive down closes in a row, we are using a 5CCD signal (5 *consecutive closes down*).

That's all there is to the basic signal and trend identification. Figures 18-1 and 18-2 show each of the signals in ideal form, and Figures 18-3 and 18-4 show them in real time on a 5-minute bar chart. As you can see, a CCU signal triggers a buy, and a CCD signal triggers a sell. Figures 18-5 and 18-6 illustrate the CCU and CCD signals on a 10-minute chart.

How the CC System Operates

The implementation of CCU and CCD signals is also a simple matter. If a 5 CCU buy signal is being used, then you *buy* the fifth higher consecutive close (see figures). You hold the position with a predetermined stop loss or you exit the long and reverse to short when you get a CCD sell signal. In practice, the number of consecutive closes which generates a buy signal will not necessarily be the same as the number of CCs which generate a sell signal.

You may use three approaches in implementing the CC system.

■ Close out positions at a specific target. The problem with this approach is that you will limit your profits. When a runaway move occurs, you

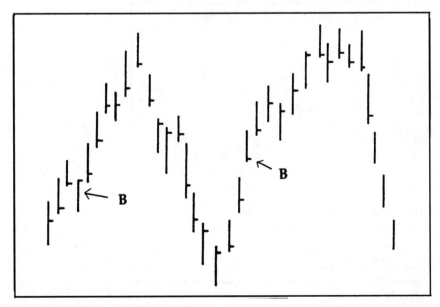

Figure 18-1. Basic CC buy signal.

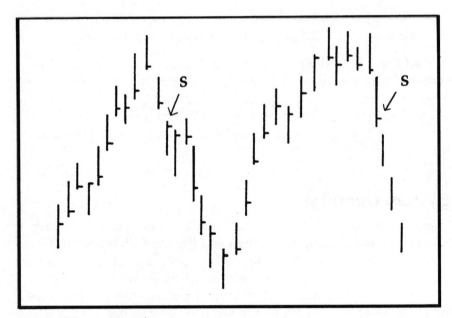

Figure 18-2. Basic CC sell signal.

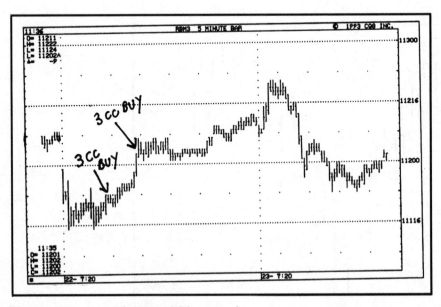

Figure 18-3. Actual 5-minute CC buy signal.

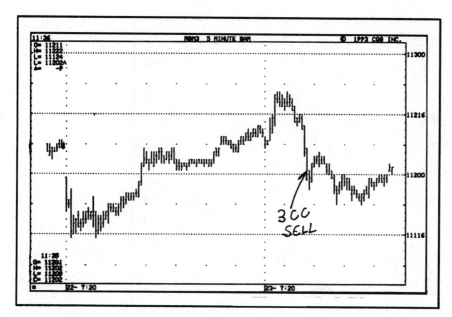

Figure 18-4. Actual 5-minute CC sell signal.

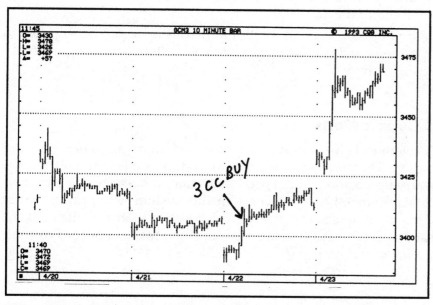

Figure 18-5. Actual 10-minute CC buy signal.

Figure 18-6. Actual 10-minute CC sell signal.

won't be on board. The successful trader must ride profits as long as possible.

■ Close out and reverse positions when a reversing signal has occurred or at the end of the day.

■ Use a trailing stop loss. You will find that using a trailing stop loss to exit positions and go flat may serve you better than using a strictly reversing system.

Summary and Conclusions

The CC method is a viable and effective technique for short-term and day trading. This technique appears to perform better on a short-term basis, carrying positions for several days, than it does strictly on a day-trade basis. Remember, however, that this system will work better at some times than others, that it will work better in more volatile markets, and that you are better off using a trailing stop loss as opposed to waiting for a reversal signal.

19

Sentiment Reigns Supreme

Perhaps the single most overlooked indicator in short-term futures trading is that of market sentiment. I have written and researched extensively on this topic. Since I first began trading in 1968 I have been fascinated with mass psychology in the stock and futures markets and with the application of market sentiment measures as objective methods in assessing trader psychology. Possibly it may have been my original occupation of clinical psychologist which attracted me so strongly to the concept of contrary opinion and market sentiment. In any case, it is an interest that has persisted through the years. Indeed, market sentiment and trader psychology have been more than mere passing interests—their application to short-term trading has served me well.

In studying market sentiment we find with few exceptions that *when the vast majority of traders expect a market to move in a given direction, it is most often true that the majority is wrong*. I won't go so far as to say that the majority is always wrong. This is not the case. In fact, *the majority can be right very frequently for brief periods*. However, my studies showed that *the more strongly the majority maintains a given opinion, whether bearish or bullish, the more likely the majority is to be wrong*.

My desire to quantify market sentiment as a measure of trader psychology led me to search far and wide for concise market sentiment data which would assist me in my short-term trading. For years, however, I was unable to find such information due to the fashion in which market sentiment data were collected and disseminated. R. Earle Hadady of Pasadena, California, deserves credit for popularizing his concepts of bullish consensus, but I found his data useless to me as a day trader, since they reached me much too late. By the time I received the data, they were almost a week old.

Although Earle did a wonderful job polling brokers, newsletter writers, and other market professionals on their sentiment, the dissemination of his data was necessarily delayed due to the mechanical process of information gathering. My inability to find prompt and accurate daily market sentiment led me, in 1987, along with several associates, to begin my own program of daily sentiment collection. The *daily sentiment index* was designed to assess traders on a daily basis regarding their bullish market sentiment on all active futures markets. Since data collection began, I have amassed a considerable historical database of daily market sentiment which I have found to be extremely helpful in short-term and day trading.

Defining *Sentiment*

Perhaps the best place to begin is with a very brief but functional definition of market sentiment. Stated very simply, *market sentiment* is a numerical assessment of the percentage of bullish or bearish opinions within a group of individuals. In this case, the individuals whose opinions are polled for my daily sentiment indicator (DSI) service are all presumed to be traders and knowledgeable about the markets. They are assessed daily by my staff, and the results of the assessment are available by 4:00 p.m. Chicago time.

On the basis of these daily sentiment indicators, we can determine the degree to which our sample of traders is bullish or bearish for each of the markets. *Daily market sentiment, therefore, is a measure of how many traders in percentage terms expect a given market to go up.* Empirically, I have found that *in most markets a daily sentiment reading of 90 percent or higher very frequently indicates that the particular market will actually move lower over the next several days or that a significant top could develop over the next several days.* Due to the very short term nature of market sentiment, its use is specifically intended for determining short-term market swings only. The DSI as I use it is *nothing more than a short-term indicator of market sentiment or emotion.*

Now that we've examined what high DSI means, let's take a look at low DSI or sentiment. I've found that when market sentiment drops to a very low level, typically 15 percent or lower, this is often an indication that the particular market is likely to establish a low within the next day or two. Frequently, markets with extremely high or low sentiment tend to make their turns very soon after the sentiment indicator has reached its extreme level.

The Daily Sentiment Index—Ideal for Short-Term Trading

Since human emotion is a very volatile aspect of the futures markets, it is subject to change dramatically from one day to the next. Whereas, the majority of our DSI sample may be extremely bullish today, they could easily reverse sentiment to extremely bearish the next day, given a drop in the market or an item of significant bearish news. *Since daily sentiment is so volatile, its application must necessarily be of an extremely short-term duration.*

Given the extreme sensitivity and responsiveness of daily sentiment, its application to short-term timing is ideal. Specifically, its use as a filter for some of the intraday techniques I have discussed in this book is superb. Consider the applications described below as important additions to every day trader's repertoire. First, however, spend a few minutes reviewing the following example of DSI application.

A Brief Historical Overview

As you know, the last 5 years have been anything but tame in S&P futures. The market has survived two severe declines, one in 1987 and another in 1990, making new all-time highs after each sharp decline. The trend has continued persistently higher with the exception of these two major corrections. The market has trekked doggedly higher, climbing a wall of worry after worry, refusing to give in to bearish fundamental after bearish fundamental. There seems to be no individual fundamental which will drive prices persistently lower.

Yet, my study of my DSI back to 1987 has revealed some extremely interesting results which I'd like to share with you. But before doing so a brief statement regarding the relationship between daily sentiment and price is in order.

Simply stated, high sentiment (i.e., about 90 percent bullish or higher) tends to signal tops, whereas low sentiment (i.e., about 15 percent or lower) tends to signal market bottoms. We're not talking here about long-term tops—we're only talking about shorter-term tops and bottoms, some lasting a few weeks, others a few days or less.

Sentiment is no more a perfect indicator than is any other market indicator. It has its shortcomings, but it also has its strong points, the most important of which is that it tends to be a *leading* indicator rather than a *lagging* indicator. *Astute traders would rather have one reliable leading indicator than 1000 semireliable or questionable lagging indicators. It's one thing to know 2 days after the fact what should have been done. It's far more meaningful to know what must be done a day, 2 days, or even 2 hours ahead of time.*

A DSI Day-Trading Application

As an example of how the DSI relates to short-term price swings in S&P futures, consider the listing in Figure 19-1. This list shows DSI readings of 90 percent or more (top expected) and 10 percent or less (bottom expected) by market, and the price change for the next several trading sessions. Take a few minutes to evaluate this list. What are your conclusions about extreme DSI readings and short-term price swings?

Visualizing Market Sentiment Relationships

Before delving into the applications of the DSI as a filter, let's first examine the ideal and actual relationships between DSI, price, tops, and bottoms.

Figure 19-2 shows the ideal relationship between market sentiment and trend. As you can see, market sentiment tends to increase with an up trend and decrease with a down trend. In fact, market sentiment very closely mimics trend in virtually every market. There are some significant instances, however, in which daily sentiment and trend differ markedly.

These are, in particular, tops and bottoms. Figure 19-3 shows the ideal relationship between DSI, market tops, and market bottoms. Compare both the ideal trend relationship from Figure 19-3 as well as the top and bottom relationship from Figure 19-3 with the actual charts shown in Figure 19-4 through 19-6. These charts are not exceptions. The fact is that a significant number of important tops occur when the DSI is at 90 percent or higher and that a significant number of bottoms occur when the DSI is at 15 percent or lower. This is an important market relationship which can be taken advantage of by the day trader. But how?

The Importance of Market Sentiment

As I've already noted, one of my favorite methods of finding potentially profitable day trades is to use daily market sentiment as a filter. Typically, when daily market sentiment is very high, markets tend to top, and when daily market sentiment is very low, i.e., bearish, markets tend to bottom. In many cases, the highs and lows in market sentiment

Date	DSI %	Price	Date	Price	Result
10/19/87	07	201.50	10/23/87	253.00H	+ As much as 5200 points to recovery high.
11/04/87	04	250.15	11/06/87	258.20H	+ About 800-point rally to next intraday high.
03/24/88	10	264.10	04/08/88	271.95H	+ Rallied about 700 points to intraday high.
03/25/88	09	257.75	04/08/88	271.95H	+ Great recovery of over 1400 points to the high.
07/12/88	09	269.35	07/15/88	273.70H	+ Smaller recovery but rallied over next 3 days.
09/14/89	09	348.30	09/19/89	353.30H	+ Another small rally following low sentiment.
11/03/89	10	339.40	11/17/89	344.20H	+ Gained about 480 points after low DSI.
11/06/89	05	333.40	11/17/89	344.20H	+ Over 1000-point gain in next few trading sessions.
06/19/90	05	363.60	06/22/90	368.45H	+ About 400-point gain possible to next high.
06/20/90	08	364.40	06/22/90	368.45H	+ Minor recovery to next high following low DSI.
07/23/90	06	357.80	07/26/90	360.35H	+ Another minor rally after low DSI.
08/16/90	09*	331.75	08/21/90	326.60H	− Clearly a losing trade in spite of low DSI.
09/27/90	07	302.70	10/02/90	323.50H	+ This one more than made up for the last one!
10/01/90	**92**	318.25	10/12/90	297.50L	+ Another beauty—dropped over 2000 points.
10/09/90	07	305.75	10/22/90	318.65H	+ Followed by a great gain to the next small top.
10/11/90	07	302.20	10/22/90	318.65H	+ Another day of low DSI confirmed a rally.
11/07/90	07	307.25	11/14/90	323.75H	+ Wow! Gained over 1600 points after low DSI.
01/14/91	06	316.85	01/17/91	339.50H	+ And yet another gain of about 2200 after low DSI.
02/04/91	**92***	351.70	02/06/91	353.50L	− This one was a small loser after a high DSI.
02/05/91	**93***	355.60	02/06/91	353.50L	− And this one lost as well in spite of 93 percent DSI.
02/13/91	**93**	373.10	02/26/91	365.90L	+ But this one did well gaining about 700 points.
02/27/91	**93**	372.30	03/19/91	368.00L	+ And this one did well too!
03/05/91	**93**	380.80	03/22/91	368.10L	+ Still another possible winner following high DSI.
03/26/91	**92**	379.70	04/10/91	372.75L	+ Fell about 700 points after high DSI.
04/16/91	**90**	389.15	04/30/91	374.20L	+ This was great too—fell nearly 1500 points.
04/17/91	**92**	392.15	04/30/91	374.20L	+ A double whammy! Big drop after 2 days, high DSI.
05/15/91	07	369.65	05/31/91	391.00H	+ Scored a major rally after very low DSI.
05/30/91	**91**	387.50	06/12/91	374.20L	+ Followed by a 1300 + drop from 91 percent DSI.

Figure 19-1. DSI extremes in S&P futures, 1982–1993.

Date	DSI %	Price	Date	Price	Result
06/12/91	05	374.20	06/14/91	382.90H	+ 5 percent DSI led to 800 + point rally to intraday high.
06/24/91	07	373.50	07/02/91	380.90H	+ Still another rally off low sentiment
07/31/91	**92**	388.40	08/06/91	385.20L	+ Not too big of a drop despite 92 percent DSI.
08/16/91	10	386.85	09/03/91	398.60H	+ Great rally of about 1100 points from 10 percent DSI.
08/19/91	08	378.85	09/03/91	398.60H	+ A double whammy after 2 days of low DSI.
11/19/91	08	380.95	11/21/91	382.15H	+ Just a tiny recovery from low sentiment.
12/26/91	**93***	407.25	01/02/92	413.80L	− This was clearly a loser without a doubt.
12/31/91	**93**	419.70	01/13/92	416.45L	+ Just a small drop after excessively high DSI.
03/05/92	08	408.85	03/19/92	412.50H	+ Small rally from low DSI.
04/08/92	08	395.25	04/16/92	417.30H	+ Fantastic rally from low DSI—over 2200 points!
05/04/92	**94**	416.50	05/15/92	410.00L	+ Dropped nicely after high DSI.
06/22/92	06	405.00	07/02/92	417.20H	+ And rallied over 1200 points from 6 percent sentiment.
10/02/92	07	409.90	10/20/92	418.00H	+ Another good one following low DSI.
10/07/92	08	403.75	10/20/92	418.00H	+ Persistently low DSI led to a rally.
10/09/92	04	403.10	10/20/92	418.00H	+ Double whammy—major rally—lowest DSI ever.
11/02/92	**96**	422.05	11/05/92	415.70L	+ Good drop after 96 percent DSI.
11/11/92	**90**	422.55	11/17/92	418.05L	+ Small drop from 90 percent DSI reading.
11/24/92	**91***	428.10	12/01/92	428.70L	− A small loser in spite of 91 percent DSI.
12/01/92	**96**	431.10	12/04/92	429.55L	+ A brief decline to the low in next few days.
12/04/92	**92**	433.55	12/16/92	431.40L	+ And another brief decline to the intraday low.
12/07/92	**93**	436.10	12/16/92	431.40L	+ But this one was quite good after high DSI.

* = DSI trades that were clearly losers.
H = High of day
L = Low of day
+ = Market move in expected direction
− = Market failed to move in expected direction.
Bold dates and DSI = High DSI readings.

Figure 19-1. DSI extremes in S&P futures, 1982–1993. *(Continued)*

correlate strongly with uncanny opportunities to enter markets at extreme lows for long positions or at extreme highs for short positions.

Many traders consider S&P futures to be a contrary market. Trading systems which work well in most other markets seem to fall apart when used in S&P futures. Market patterns which are known to be reliable in

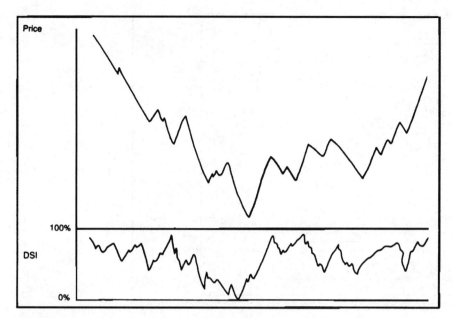

Figure 19-2. Ideal relationship between trend and DSI.

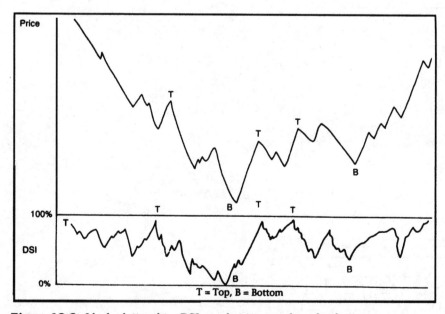

Figure 19-3. Ideal relationship: DSI, market tops, and market bottoms.

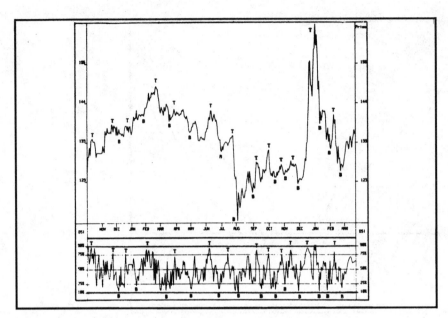

Figure 19-4. Actual example of DSI versus price.

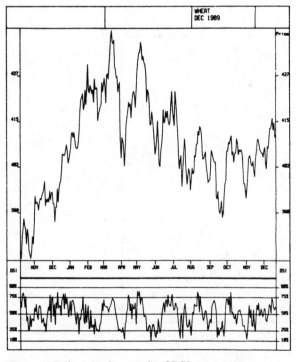

Figure 19-5. Actual example of DSI versus price.

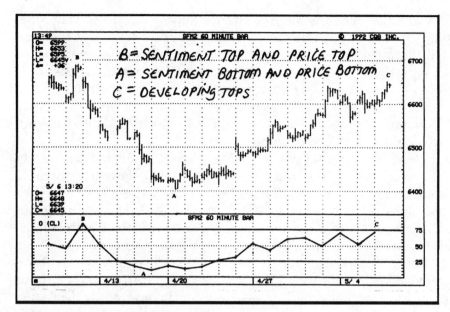

Figure 19-6. Actual example of DSI versus price.

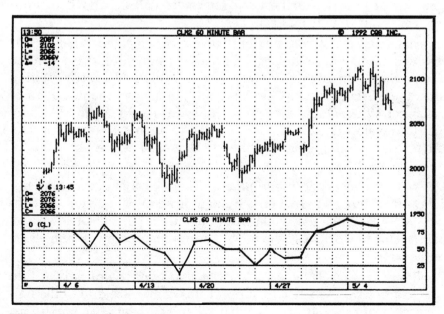

Figure 19-6. (*Continued*)

virtually all other markets are like strangers to S&P futures. Why does this happen? Although I'm not entirely sure, I do have my theories. Perhaps the most cogent reason is that the S&P futures market is a hybrid, representing both stocks and futures. The market is monitored closely by computers and money managers for imbalances. Furthermore, it is used heavily as a hedging vehicle by stock fund managers. Although it is a speculative market, it is affected by a host of variables which do not affect most other markets.

Yet there is one variable which seems to work better in S&P futures than in any other market—and that's daily market sentiment. Because S&P is such a liquid market (most of the time), because it is followed by stock and futures traders, because it is heavily traded by professionals from all sectors of the financial arena, because it is the quintessential speculators market, and because it has a high dollar value per tick, it is a market which is more sensitive to trader emotion than any other futures market in existence today. And this is all very comforting to those of us who enjoy having reliable indicators to assist us in our trading decisions.

- *DSI with gap signals of both types.* One of my favorite applications of the market sentiment as assessed by the DSI is with gap trades. It is not uncommon for the best gap trades to occur in close proximity to extreme sentiment readings. As you can easily imagine, your best odds for *buy gap trades* of both types is when sentiment is at or about 15 percent or lower. Your best *sell gap trades* will occur when sentiment is at about 90 percent or higher.

- *MA channel and DSI are also an outstanding combination.* When DSI is excessively high, you can expect an MAC sell signal to develop on the intraday charts. In such cases you can feel relatively secure selling against the MAH as well as the MAL and, of course, the midpoint of the channel. When DSI is excessively low you can expect an MAC buy signal to develop on the intraday charts. In such cases you can feel relatively secure buying against the MAH as well as the MAL and, of course, the midpoint of the channel.

- *Stochastic pop signals can also be filtered using DSI.* I suggest caution if you get an SP buy signal when sentiment is about 90 percent or higher or a sell SP sell signal when DSI is about 15 percent or lower. SP signals seems to work best when DSI has not reached an extreme level on either side.

- *Critical time of day (CTOD) signals also appear to be related to DSI.* I do not have any hard evidence to support this conjecture due to the limited number of cases. It appears that when DSI is at a high extreme, CTOD sell signals will be more reliable. When DSI is at a low extreme,

CTOD buy signals tend to work better. (See Chapter 20 for discussion of CTOD methods.)

- *Oscillator signals, as discussed in a previous chapter, can also be filtered with DSI.* When DSI is too high, oscillator buy signals are apt to be unreliable whereas oscillator sell signals are more likely to work well for larger moves. Conversely, when DSI is too low, you should be careful about taking sell signals, since oscillator buy signals tend to be more accurate and they tend to produce larger moves.

In the final analysis, market sentiment can be used as an excellent filter for the many different day-trading methods and systems I've discussed in this book. Daily market sentiment is subject to such wide swings because it is based on trader response, which is, in turn, based on trader perception of market events. Trader perception is mediated by emotion. Hence, DSI is an excellent indicator of emotion. Since many large intraday price moves are based on emotion, DSI is an excellent method for determining markets which are in an emotional state sufficiently conducive to reliable intraday moves. That's why I urge all day traders to be aware of and to use daily market sentiment.

DSI Historical Data

I have been collecting daily market sentiment data since 1987. The historical database is sufficiently extensive now to allow for fairly intensive research. Although I am constantly researching ways of using DSI data for day trading as well as short-term and position trading, I do not have all the answers with regard to using this powerful tool. For those who wish to do their own research (and I encourage this), I am making the historical data available at no charge whatsoever either in hard copy printout or on computer disk. If you would like to obtain the data then simply send me a blank disk along with a stamped, self-addressed envelope (about 3-oz postage). For a hard copy printout, send a stamped self-addressed envelope (about 7-oz postage). If you have questions about the data, please don't hesitate to contact my office (MBH Commodity Advisors, Inc., P.O. Box 353, Winnetka, Ill. 60093). I am glad to provide the historical data at no charge, since it will stimulate more research on this valuable indicator.

Daily updates of the DSI are provided via hotline, fax, or computer bulletin board. There is a subscription fee for this service, since I do have costs in gathering and disseminating the data daily.

20
Critical Time of Day (CTOD)

Perhaps one of the most interesting and intriguing day-trading methods is what I call *critical time of day* (CTOD). This is a method I've been using since the late 1970s when I first developed it. It is both simple and easily applied, yet it is demanding inasmuch as it requires the trader to be present throughout the day, tracking prices every 5 minutes. This is why the method may not be suitable for all traders.

The CTOD method has remained virtually unchanged since it was developed. This is a strong testimonial to its efficacy. I caution you, however, to remember that CTOD is a method, *it is not a system*, although it is systematic and has the potential to be used as a system. CTOD is designed to spot intraday price moves based on the 5-minute closing price range during the first 2 hours of the trading day.

Basic CTOD Signals and Parameters

The basic methodology and operational procedures for using CTOD measures are as follows:

■ Plot the 5-minute closing prices for the first 2 hours of trading regardless of market (see exceptions later on). By 5-minute closing prices, I mean the price at the end of every 5 minutes. The price used is the last price, not the intraday high or low price. When plotted according to the rules, the 5-minute closing price plot for the first 2 hours of trading will look like Figure 20-1. See also Figure 20-2 for ideal buy-and-sell signals the same day.

> *Remember this, it is important. Use the price at the end of each 5 minutes, not the high or low, but the last price each 5 minutes.*

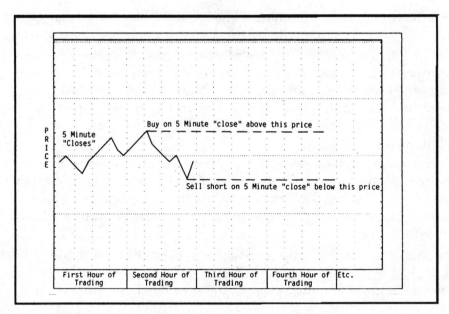

Figure 20-1. First 2 hours of closing prices—ideal example.

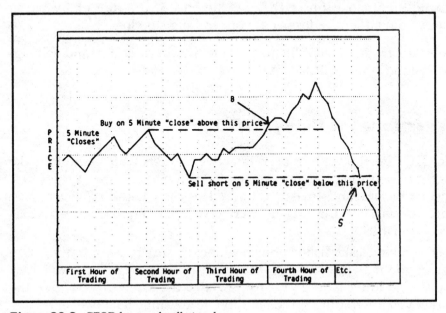

Figure 20-2. CTOD buy-and-sell signals.

- Once the first 2 hours of 5-minute closing price data have been gathered, the highest price will be used as a buying breakout point, whereas the lowest price will be used as a selling breakout point.

- An upper breakout and *buy signal* will occur when prices have had a 5-minute "close" (i.e., plot) above the highest 5-minute closing plot established during the first 2 hours. You will then buy at the market using a 5-minute closing stop loss below the lowest closing 5-minute plot of the first 2 hours.

- A lower breakout and *sell signal* will occur when prices have had a 5-minute close (i.e., plot) below the lowest 5-minute closing plot established during the first 2 hours. You will then sell at the market using a 5-minute closing stop loss above the highest closing 5-minute plot of the first 2 hours.

- You will use a trailing stop loss which consists of a 5-minute close below the lowest 5-minute close of each previous hour for longs and above the highest 5-minute close of the previous hour for short positions.

- As an alternative you can use a money management stop loss or a stop loss based on other indicators discussed in this book (e.g., moving averages or oscillators).

- You will exit positions either by the end of the day or by being stopped out either at a loss or at your trailing stop loss.

Figures 20-3 through 20-5 illustrate some examples of buy-and-sell signals using the 2-hour CTOD parameters.

Tips and Suggestions for Using CTOD

✓ The CTOD method is best used in active markets which tend to make large moves during the day. Currently such markets are S&P futures, most currencies, and Treasury bonds. This can change, however, inasmuch as markets currently not active will one day become active as well as volatile.

✓ Once you have established your position, be sure to use a trailing stop loss, or you may find your profit rapidly diminishing. The whole idea of CTOD trading is to grab profits yet at the same time to give the market you are trading sufficient room to continue its move.

✓ Experiment with different time frames such as 1 hour, or $1\frac{1}{2}$ hours. Study the markets you are trading for unique characteristics which allow short- or long-time windows to work better.

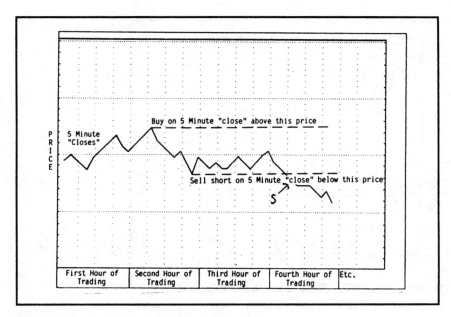

Figure 20-3. A CTOD sell signal.

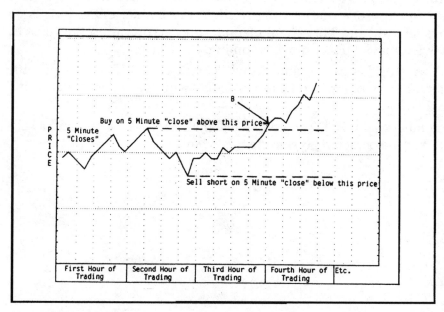

Figure 20-4. A CTOD buy signal.

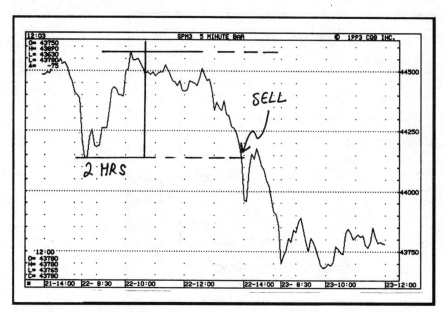

Figure 20-5. Another CTOD signal.

✓ Multiple units can offer you the best of possible worlds using CTOD. If, for example, you enter your initial position with two units, then you can close one out at a profit when the market either bulges or drops sharply and hold the remaining unit according to the rules in the event that a further move is coming.

✓ Trailing stop losses can and do work with CTOD. Experiment with different stop loss methods, in particular with those described in this book.

✓ Remember that CTOD can give two signals each day, a buy and a sell, or it may, on occasion give no signals whatsoever.

21

Putting It All Together

Now that you've had an opportunity to review and study the many systems, methods, and indicators I've presented in this book, the ultimate issue must be addressed, and that is, *How do you put all of it together into a profitable trading strategy?* The question appears simple and straightforward, but the answer is, unfortunately, not so simple. Because traders differ so markedly in their expectations, abilities, and available time, it is not possible to state categorically that any one particular strategy or methodology is more favorable or desirable than another. This is something that the individual trader will need to address on his or her own. I will, nevertheless, give you some suggestions based on my experiences, hoping that they will be meaningful to you and that, perhaps you will find them useful in day-trading futures profitably. Unfortunately, I can make no guarantees, and even if I could, I would be prohibited from doing so by the existing regulatory agencies. I will, however, guarantee you the following:

> *If you learn and apply consistent trading rules and indicators to the markets on a day-trading basis, you will achieve profitable results so long as you remain consistent, well capitalized, and willing to accept losses when they should be accepted.*

With this caveat in mind, I will now review some valuable suggestions based on my considerable experiences as a trader. Please note that this list is not necessarily in chronological order, nor is it in order of importance.

Before You Begin Day Trading.   Perhaps you are already day trading or trading for the short term. If this is the case, and if you are not pleased with your results, then I suggest you stop what you are doing and consider some of the suggestions and methods proposed in this book. I think it is important for you to find trading techniques not only which appeal to you from the standpoint of logic, but which also are consistent with your abilities as a trader. If, for example, you have a full-time job which does not allow you to follow the markets tick by tick or every 5 or 10 minutes within the day, then clearly many of the techniques in this book are not suitable for you. You would want to restrict your trading possibly to such techniques as the two gap methods I have discussed. However, if you are able to sit and watch the market on an intraday basis, then you must find those techniques which appeal to you and which are also consistent with your abilities as a trader. You may not, for example, wish to watch the markets tick by tick in order to trade on the support and resistance methods presented in this book; rather you may wish to trade such techniques as the intraday pop. If this is the case, then it is entirely possible using certain trading software to set indicator alerts which will inform you when such signals have occurred. Certainly this is also possible in terms of identifying when certain support or resistance levels have been touched. A number of online trading software programs will allow you to achieve this goal.

If You Are Already an Active Trader.   If you are already day trading, then examine the techniques presented in this book for ideas and methods or indicators and suggestions which may help you improve upon what you are doing. If, however, you are already totally satisfied with your techniques, then I would be the first to suggest that you not alter them substantially. If you feel that there is potential for you to profit using my suggestions, indicators, and methods, then I strongly recommend opening a separate day-trading account in order to implement these ideas in a fashion which does not interfere or confound what you are already doing.

Prepare for Your Day.   Although I prefer to prepare for my trading day early each morning, some traders are not able to do this or prefer making their preparations the day before either after market closings or in the evening. Either approach is acceptable as long as there is some degree of organization and preparation in what you are doing. I have found that many of my trading blunders occur when I make impulsive decisions. This is not to say that unplanned-for decisions cannot be made during the day; however, it is important for traders to have a very general overview of what to do the next day.

For those who are trading the gap systems, the preparatory work is very clear indeed. Go through the markets prior to opening (either the night before or that very day) and find those markets which have closed very close to their low price for the day or very close to their high price for the day. Jot down market and contract month and watch these markets for possible gap openings the next day. This will allow you to prepare for possible trades and to filter out those markets in which you will have no day-trading interest due to either their lack of volatility, thin trading volume, or characteristically small price moves. Do not assume that any given market is an unfit candidate for gap trades. Frequently, markets which have been known as sleepers spring to life following an opening price gap.

Support and resistance may also be determined in advance using the MAC method and the intraday charts. I strongly suggest that you do this work in advance as well. As you can see, my preference is to study the markets in advance whether for potential signals, developing chart patterns, or to find approaching support and/or resistance levels.

Determine If Any Important Reports Are Scheduled.   Although many traders enjoy the thrill of watching markets respond to major government reports and/or news items, I am not impressed by the above and actually prefer avoiding the markets until the dust has settled following the release of such reports. Market response may create certain trading opportunities, but I think that the average trader is far better off waiting until the news has been digested and then entering his or her day trades.

I have found that those trading signals which occur after the first hour of trading, after overnight news has been assimilated, after important reports have been released, and after the trading participants have had an opportunity to express their sentiment by buying or selling tend to be more reliable. I have also found that signals which occur toward the last 1 to 2 hours of each trading session tend to be more reliable. I have no hard statistical evidence to support this assertion or observation, but I urge you to study the markets and make your own observations.

Keep Good Records.   I would be a much richer man today had I learned in my early days as a trader that good record keeping is important, especially for the day trader. As an active trader, the day-to-day necessities of tracking your positions, making certain your price fills are correct as reported by your broker, making certain you remember to cancel and/or replace certain orders, and making certain that your orders have been filled, are very, very important. Errors occur frequently and must be corrected immediately, otherwise they may prove costly.

I suggest you either use a trading card such as those used on the exchange floor, or construct yourself a spreadsheet such as the one shown in Figure 21-1. Better yet, track your positions on a computer spreadsheet which you may easily design yourself in any of the popular spreadsheet programs.

Your record-keeping system need not be elaborate. It need only be highly functional. When an order has been filled, check the order off. When an order has been canceled, cross the order out. When an order has been canceled and replaced, indicate so. Make sure you enter order numbers on your spreadsheet. An order number will be given to you by your broker (in most cases) when the order is placed. This will simplify the search process when attempting to discover if an order has been filled or in canceling an order. This is especially important for extremely active day traders. Ask your broker to give you an order number each time you place an order.

Also jot down the exact time you placed your order or use one of the many popular time stamping machines and actually write an order ticket for each order you place. You may think that this is an unnecessarily detailed or compulsive procedure, but believe me, it is not. For those of you who have seen my office, this close attention to detail may seem an incongruity in my personality. It may very well be, yet I find it necessary in order to preserve and protect my account from costly errors. Organization and good record keeping are extremely important for the day trader.

Check your positions every day before trading begins. Make certain that your orders from the day before have been executed correctly as

L/S	Mkt/Mo	Price In	Active Order(s)	Price Out	Profit/Loss	Notes

Figure 21-1. Sample daily trading record.

given and at the correct prices, namely the prices which were reported back to you. Report any changes, omissions, and/or corrections and errors to your broker immediately! The longer you wait, the more likely it will be that the error will be yours regardless of whose it actually was. Some brokerage firms offer a preliminary position run at the end of the trading day for their active traders. This run is downloaded by computer and may be printed out at your office frequently before 4:00 p.m. Chicago time. For those of you who are extremely active traders, such a preliminary run will prove very helpful. In addition to the spreadsheet or trading card that I recommended, a number of commercially available electronic notepads small enough to fit in your pocket will do the job quite well.

Check your orders frequently during the day to make sure that you have not forgotten to cancel an order or that you have not neglected to jot down an order number. All this may seem somewhat unnecessary to you, but I can assure you that it will pay off not only in the short run but in the long run as well. I cannot overemphasize the importance of good record keeping as a basic building block for successful day trading.

Placing Orders Promptly and Correctly. I have already reviewed with you previously my suggestions, explanations, and caveats about order placement. Unless you are a very experienced trader who is already familiar with all the terminology and with the applicability of different trading orders to different types of markets and for different purposes, then I urge you to review my definitions and suggested applications. Correct order placement is absolutely crucial to successful day trading. Review order placement and make certain that you are communicating correctly with your broker. An incorrect order will be costly in many cases.

Avoid Extraneous Input. I have stressed the importance of this behavior throughout the book. The day trader is constantly being barraged by a plethora of extraneous inputs which can achieve virtually no useful purpose other than to distract, dissuade, confuse, or intimidate. I suggest, therefore, that you keep extraneous information to a minimum, not allowing it to impinge upon your space or to infringe upon your trading decisions. In the vast majority of cases, decisions which are affected by extraneous input will not prove profitable. With the exception of specific instances which may prove beneficial, e.g., taking advantage of news to exit or enter a position as previously discussed, extraneous input is the enemy of most day traders and should be kept to the absolute minimum. Some day traders benefit from reading certain publications, paying attention to the news, or consulting the opening market indications, but I find that such information is frequently not productive and unfortunately counterproductive in many cases.

Keep a Trading Diary.   Another little device which has helped me considerably over the years is my trading diary. While this may again seem an unnecessary and compulsive preoccupation, I assure you it is anything but compulsive. I have found that the maintenance of a detailed trading diary, particularly for those who are new to day trading, can be one of the most effective learning tools available to the day trader. Your diary should contain a list of all trades that were made, the reason or reasons that you entered these trades, the reason or reasons that you exited these trades, and any other comments, particularly of an emotional undertone, which may have affected your trading decisions. This diary should be available for review and should in fact be reviewed at least once daily, preferably at the end of each trading session or previous to the next trading session early in the day so that you may relive both your trading errors as well as your trading successes. The review will help you learn and will therefore increase your winning behaviors while decreasing your losing behaviors. It can also help you learn a great deal about the trading systems or techniques which you are using, whether they are the ones suggested in this book or otherwise.

22

The Psychology
of Day Trading

Perhaps the single most important aspect of any trading methodology, whether for the long term, intermediate term, short term, or day trade, is the psychology of the trader. My work with trader psychology dates back to the first trade I ever made in 1968. Having been trained as a clinical psychologist, and having practiced as such for quite a few years, I am very familiar with the limitations of the trader and with the psychological road blocks which traders constantly throw in their own paths. My book, *The Investor's Quotient* (Wiley, New York, 1980), published in 1980, has continued to be a best-seller through the years, indicating *not necessarily that my writing skills are tremendous but rather that traders realize their limitations and seek to know more about how to overcome them.*

There are those who will disagree with me, but I feel strongly that this chapter is possibly the most important one in the entire book. While many of you may choose to either ignore what I have said in this chapter or skip it entirely, I do sincerely believe that *to do so would be the worst mistake you can make.* Although it is impossible to completely discuss in one chapter what takes several books to explain thoroughly, I will do my best to acquaint you with the pitfalls which await you as a day trader.

Day traders are in the unique position of having a very short term relationship with the market. For many years day trading has been considered to be the most speculative of speculative trading activities. I believe that this is a market myth that has been perpetuated by those who are unable to day trade or who are afraid to do so. The fact of the matter is that the day trader is in an advantageous position. The true day trader understands the limitations of what can be achieved within the day time frame. The day trader is, therefore, the sharpshooter of futures trading. The day trader is interested in finding the correct target, taking aim at it, pulling the trigger, and bagging the prey. As mercenary as this may sound, that's what day trading is all about. The effective day trader will keep his or her powder dry, will aim only at the most promising targets, and will aim only at targets which are likely to be hit.

The day trader must be consistent, efficient, adaptable, and persistent. These are the most important qualities that a day trader can develop. Because day trading is unique among the many different avenues which are open to futures traders, day trading has its unique brand of psychology. In this chapter I will attempt to acquaint you with the major issues that face the day trader and, moreover, to suggest to you methods which may be used to overcome your limitations, and to maximize your strong points.

A Successful Day Trader Needs Discipline

Before we examine the psychological and behavioral issues that limit success in day trading, let's examine the qualities which facilitate or enhance day-trading results. The first among these is *discipline*. Certainly by now you've heard the word *discipline* hundreds if not thousands of times. It is probably one of the most worn out terms in all futures trading. The problem is that merely saying the word is one thing, but understanding its true definition operationally, or on a behavioral level, is a far more important thing. *What do I mean by discipline?*

- Discipline is not just the ability to develop a trading plan and to stay with it, it is also the ability to know when your trading plan is not working and, therefore, knowing when to abandon it.

- Discipline is also the ability to give your day-trading positions sufficient time to work in your favor or, for that matter, sufficient time to work against you.

- Discipline is the ability to trade again once you've take a loss. It is the ability to ignore extraneous information and to avoid inputs which are not related to the system you are using.

- Discipline is the ability to maintain reasonable position size and to avoid the motion which leads to overtrading.

- Discipline is the persistence required to maintain your trading systems and to calculate the necessary timing indicators consistently during the day, either manually or by computer.

- Above all, however, discipline is the ability to come back to the trading arena every day, regardless of whether you have won, lost, or broken even the day before.

You can see, therefore, that discipline consists of many different things. Discipline is not any one particular skill. Perhaps the best way to understand trading discipline is to examine some of its component behaviors. Let's look at a few of these.

Persistence

This is, perhaps, the single most important of all qualities that a trader can possess. Day trading, and for that matter all futures trading, is an endeavor which requires the ability to continue trading even when results have not been good. Due to the nature of markets and trading systems, bad times are frequently followed by good times, and good times are frequently followed by bad. *Some of a trader's greatest successes will occur following a string of losses.* This is why it is extremely important for traders to be persistent in applying their trading methods and to continue using them for a reasonable period. Those who quit too soon will not be in the markets when their systems begin to work; those who quit too late will run out of trading capital. Therefore, while persistence is important, it is also important to know when a trader has been too patient when it is time to quit and not play any longer using the system which you have been using.

If persistence is so important, then how does the trader develop it? The answer is simple, but the implementation is not. Persistence is developed by being persistent. Although this may sound to you like a circular answer, it is truly not. *The only way to be persistent is to force yourself initially to do everything which must be done according to the dictates of your systems or method.* Try this, if you're having difficulty. Make a commitment to a trading system or method. Follow through with that approach for a specific amount of time taking every trade according to the rules or, if the system is subjective, attempting to trade the system with as much consistency as possible. If you have been consistent in applying your rules, then you will find that, in most cases, your consistency will have paid off, and you will have profits to show for your efforts. Even if your trading was not successful, you will have learned a great deal. You will have learned that you can follow a system or method, that you can trade in a disciplined fashion, and, moreover, that the only way to do so is to be persistent by following as many of the trades and rules as possible.

Compare this to the ignorance and confusion which come from haphazard trading or by applying trading rules inconsistently. Think back to your experiences as a trader. Remember your worst losing trades. You will find that *those losses which have been taken according to a system or method are easier to accept psychologically, whereas those which have not been accepted according to the rules have often turned into terrible monsters, ultimately costing you much, much more than they should have, financially as well as psychologically.* If you would like to master the skill of persistence, then you will need to practice it. Make the commitment and I think you will see some wonderful results, even over the short term.

Willingness to Accept Losses

Here is yet another important quality that the effective day trader must either possess, acquire, or develop. Perhaps the single greatest downfall of all traders is the inability to take a loss when it should be taken. Losses have a nasty habit of becoming worse rather than better. Unless they are taken when they should be, the results will not be to your liking.

Although it is easier for the day trader to take a loss than it is for the position trader (since a loss must be accepted by the end of the trading day), it is still the downfall of many a day trader who is unwilling to accept the loss when it is a reasonable one. The good day trader must have the ability to take a loss when the time to take that loss is right. What's right is dictated by the particular trading system or risk management technique which is being used. I would venture to say from my experience and observations that *perhaps 75 percent or more of all large losses are due to the fact that losses were not taken when they were small or relatively small or when they should have been taken.*

I can certainly speak from experience when I say that my largest loss ever resulted from the fact that *I refused to take the loss when the time was right.* I allowed a $500 loss to turn into a $5000 loss. Fortunately, that was the first and last time I was guilty of that serious a transgression. Unfortunately, many traders, a great many traders in fact, refuse to take losses when the time is right. Fortunately, the day trader has two opportunities to take a loss. *The first one is at the stop loss point as determined by a system or at the predetermined dollar risk stop. The second point is at the end of the day.* A day trader is, therefore, fortunate inasmuch as he or she is forced to liquidate all positions at the end of the day. This will keep losses smaller than they would be if losing positions were carried overnight.

Here are some suggestions as to how you may improve your ability to take losses when they should be taken:

1. *Formulate your stop loss rules very specifically.* Do this whether they relate to systems or dollar risk amount, and type or write your rules in large print. Place the hard copy close to your quotation equipment, the computer which you use for trading, or the telephone from which you place your orders. If you do not use a computer or quotation sys-

tem for your trades, then please keep your rule handy on an index card and refer to it frequently during the day.

2. *Make the commitment to accept your next 10 losses completely as dictated by your system.* Once you have done this, the behavior will become habitual and losses will be easier to accept.

3. *If you trade with a full-service broker or a trading partner, make your broker or partner aware of where your stop loss will be.* Have them remind you that you must exit your position accordingly. You may wish to give them the authority to do so for you, assuming of course, that your relationship with them is sufficiently close to allow for such a procedure.

4. *Place your stop loss.* A much more simple procedure, although I do not necessarily recommend it at all times due to the nature of day trading, is to actually place your stop loss as soon as your entry order has been filled.

These suggestions will, I feel, help you master the ability to take losses in a timely and rational fashion.

The Ability to Avoid Overtrading

Too many day traders feel that they must trade every day. Let's face it, some traders are addicted to trading. A day without a trade for them is like a day without a meal. The fact is that there are some days which offer few if any trading opportunities. *The day trader who wishes to preserve capital and avoid losses as well as unnecessary commission charges should understand that day trading is not an everyday event.* There will be days when no trades are indicated. Believe me when I tell you that things are better that way.

One of the telltale signs of the day trader about to go astray is the searching-for-a-good-trade syndrome. Have you ever found yourself sitting at the computer or quotation screen, bored because there have been no trades that day? Have you ever found your fingers idly rambling over the keyboard searching chart after chart looking for markets to trade? *Yes, my friend, this is the first sign of trouble.* Should you ever find yourself in this position, *do yourself a favor and stop looking.* Good day-trading opportunities within the parameters I have set forth in this book are plentiful, but they do not occur every day. Consequently, set yourself standards as to which markets you will day trade, and if there are no day trades in these markets do not allow yourself to endlessly wander about the keyboard looking for day trades in such things as orange juice or palladium. They may work for you from time to time, but the odds of success are very slim. Take my word for it, the successful day trader will specialize in only a handful of markets and will do well at these. Do not attempt to spread yourself too thin by looking for trading opportunities where in fact they do not exist. And this brings me to my next point.

The Ability to Specialize

Successful day trading is a time-consuming undertaking which requires close attention. In many cases it require diligence, follow-through, and persistence. Although some day-trading techniques I have discussed in this book, specifically the gap methods, lend themselves to strictly mechanical trading, many do not. It will be possible for you to enter orders for gap trades without watching the markets closely. However, the vast majority of techniques require close attention. Therefore it is unfeasible for most day traders to be involved in too many markets at one time. I suggest that day trading three markets is sufficient for the majority of traders. In fact, for new day traders, I would recommend specializing in only one market, attending to this market thoroughly and carefully in order to develop your skills and to increase your overall profits.

What should the new day trader trade? Naturally, the answer to this question will change as a function of market conditions. Some markets historically have lent themselves well to day trading—the currencies, S&P futures, and Treasury bonds. However, some markets such as silver, soybeans, the petroleum complex markets, and other currencies make good day-trading vehicles as well under certain market conditions. Consequently, I would pay attention to these as well when they become sufficiently active and volatile. In terms of gap trades, there are many markets which are good day-trading vehicles inasmuch as entry will be on a specifically defined buy or sell stop with exit usually on the close of trading. Since gap trades do not in many cases require close attention, many markets may be day traded in this fashion. For the newcomer, however, I would recommend a very limited portfolio of trades until techniques have been mastered and self-confidence has been achieved.

Beginning with Sufficient Capital

Perhaps one of the worst blunders that any trader could commit whether trading from the day time frame or from a position trade perspective is to attempt trading with insufficient capital. The argument may be made that the day trader does not need to have substantial capital in his or her account since trades are closed out at the end of the day and therefore the necessity for sufficient margin to maintain positions is eliminated. While this may be true, it is also true that those with limited funds cannot play the game as long as those with larger funds can. It is important in any venture to start with sufficient capital in order that the trader not feel pressured to perform and to allow the particular trading system or methods sufficient opportunity to ride through periods of poor performance.

The trader with limited capital will not only be a nervous trader, looking always to minimize losses beyond the point of realistic trading, but also will frequently be knocked out of the game after a series of losses, before his or her trading methods have had the opportunity to perform. Consequently, capitalize your trading account sufficiently or decide ahead of time that you will trade only a very limited portfolio consistent with your available capital. Do not start with an undercapitalized account, since this is a near certain invitation to failure. In order to begin trading with sufficient capital the aspiring trader will have to be realistic and, above all, patient enough to gather the speculative capital which will be needed.

The Ability to Use News to Your Advantage

Many a trader has learned the hard way that following the news can frequently lead to losses. I have discovered that there are ways in which the trader may use the fundamental news or developing international, domestic, or political news to his or her advantage. To use the news in your favor, *do not be a follower of the news, rather be a "fade" of the news.* Use the news to exit positions which you have most likely established well before the news has become public knowledge. I am a firm believer in the old market dictum: *buy on rumor, sell on news.* On an intraday basis, markets are very sensitive to news well before the news is known by most traders. Insiders buy and sell on expectation, sometimes based on rumor, frequently based on fact. They establish positions before the general public is aware of the news, and, once the news has become public knowledge, they take advantage of the surge or the drop in prices to exit positions.

Therefore, if you wish to use the news to your advantage, you must be a contrarian. This is especially true from the day-trading perspective. Although there is nothing wrong with following intraday trends, frequently intraday trends react strongly to news developments. If you are following your trading system or method, you will most often be on the correct side of the market when such news develops. Take advantage of price surges or declines to exit your position. This require self-control and the ability to see the news as your opportunity to get out, not as you opportunity to hold on for even more profit!

Taking Advantage of Brief Price Surges

In order to day trade profitably, you must also learn to take advantage of brief flurries in prices. In the previous section I discussed large intra-day price moves which can occur in relation to international, domestic, political, and economic news. At times, markets will drop or rally quickly seemingly in response to no news. What may be happening in such cases is a rumor on the trading floor, a large buyer or buy order, or large seller or sell order of which you are not aware. Such brief price surges or drops are opportunities for you to exit positions consistent with the price move.

Regardless of the source, consider all price rallies or declines which occur quickly within the day's trading session to be an opportunity for you to either exit your current position at a profit, or to establish a new position using support and resistance methods which have been out-lined previously. It is important to develop this quality as a day trader, since it is entirely consistent with the day-trading objective. Too many day traders assume that bulges or sharp declines in price within the day are basically meaningless. Believe me they're not. They're tailor-made for the day trader. The day trader who is committed to taking a profit out of the market every day must take advantage of these price moves. If you decide not to do so, then by all means you must either raise or lower your stop loss (depending on your position), or you must use an appropriate mental stop loss which is adjusted to the change in price. What this means simply is use a trailing stop loss in the event that the price move is negated shortly after it begins. In this way you will have given yourself an opportunity to lock in a larger profit which you might not otherwise have had.

Sticking to Your Daily Goal

Above all remember that as a day trader you have one major goal and that is to make money trading each day. The important consideration here is that in order to make money day trading every day you will need to be particularly aware of your net profits during the day (after costs) and as the day progresses if you are riding profits. You will be more inclined to take those profits in order to make each day profitable.

My advice, which is based on many years of short-term and day trading, is to set yourself specific standards regarding when you will begin to liquidate positions toward the end of the day in order to guarantee yourself a profitable day. My advice is to do so approximately 1 hour before the close of trading. You may either begin to close out your positions at that time or you may use a follow-up stop loss procedure in order to "lock in" existing profits.

Many traders would disagree with my advice. As I indicated earlier, however, it is based on many years of trading experience, and it is designed to achieve a very important goal for the day trader. As a day trader you need to end each day with a profit, no matter how small that profit may be. If you can do so, you will be reinforced positively for your day-trading skills. This will give you confidence and a positive attitude toward your trading profession which, of course, is very important, particularly when you have experienced a string of losses. In other words, if you can be even slightly successful each day, your attitude toward day trading will become more positive, your self-confidence will increase, and you will be more able to withstand the temporary reversal to which all traders, short-term, long-term, and day traders alike, frequently fall victim.

But in order to achieve this goal you will need to internalize it, keeping it foremost in your mind at all times. What is right and proper for the position trader or for the short-term trader is not necessarily good for the day trader. If you find yourself wanting to ride profits or losses overnight, then you are not being true to your goal as a day trader. Should you wish to day trade and position trade as well then I urge you to do so in different accounts in order to avoid the confusion which will assuredly come from doing both in the same account. Keep your goal in mind, and you will be less likely to stray from it.

Using Market Sentiment to Find Day-Trading Opportunities

I have already discussed the importance of going against the majority opinion in order to find profitable day-trading opportunities. *I believe that this is one of the most important qualities a day trader can possess.* While there is certainly a great deal of money to be made day trading with the existing trend, *it is also important to know when the existing trend has reached a possible turning point.* One of the best ways if not the best way of doing this is through the use of market sentiment. Since I have already discussed the particulars of applying market sentiment for the purposes of day trading, I will not repeat this information here; however, I do again stress its importance. *The day trader must also be a contrarian*. This does not mean that you must buck the trend, but it *does mean that you must always be aware of whether sentiment is very high or very low*. This will give you important clues as to whether you should be quick to take profits, whether you can allow profits to run, and whether you should look for trading opportunities on the opposite side of the existing trend.

Conclusion

Although there are many other important qualities that a successful day trader must either possess or acquire, I believe I have covered the most significant ones. If you strive to develop these qualities, *then your odds of success as a day trader will certainly be better*. I have learned, after my many years of trading, that *the major difference between those who are successful traders and those who are not is to be found in their psychological make-up and in the skills they have acquired as traders rather than in the trading systems they use*.

Although it is certainly helpful to have an effective trading system, even the best trading system in the hands of an undisciplined trader is nothing more than a destructive tool. Consequently, you must develop your skills as a day trader along the guidelines I have given you in this chapter.

Occasionally, traders will have idiosyncratic difficulties in the markets which must be addressed on an individual basis. If this is the case, then I suggest you identify your particular problem as succinctly as you can and, if you cannot formulate a good method for minimizing the problems which this behavior causes you, I suggest you contact a professional for assistance. If you are not successful in your search for help, please drop me a line and I may have some helpful suggestions for you (MBH Commodity Advisors, Inc., P.O. Box 353, Winnetka, Ill. 60093).

23

The Impact of 24-Hour Trading on Day Trading

Increased activity in the European futures markets as well as 24-hour futures trading through the Globex system has had a significant impact on the U.S. futures markets. Some day traders are concerned that these influences will adversely affect their systems, methods, procedures, and profits. I disagree. As long as we remain cognizant that markets are now globally traded on a round-the-clock basis, we can adjust our methods accordingly. Here are some suggestions and observations regarding the European markets and 24-hour trading with respect to your role as a day trader:

1. First let me define what I mean by the *European markets.* Time will certainly alter my list, but I mean primarily the markets traded at the London International Financial Futures Exchange (LIFFE) and the MATIF exchange in Paris. The specific markets which I find extremely reliable using the indicators and methods in this book are Gilt, Bund, Italian Bond, EuroMark, Short Sterling, FTSE 100, Pibor, CAC40, DAX, and Notionell Bond.

2. The systems, methods, and indicators discussed in this book appear to be effective in all markets no matter what their geographic location. As examples consider Figures 23-1 through 23-5, which illustrate a number of the indicators discussed in the preceding chapters. From all indications these methods work just as well, if not better, in the European markets.

3. When using the gap trading system on the currency, stock index, and interest rate futures markets, which are traded overnight in the

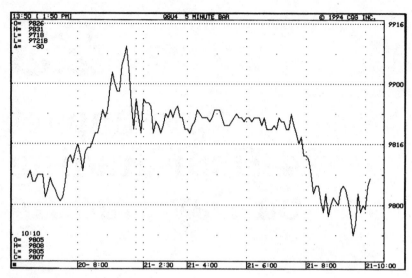

Figure 23-1. Critical time of day (CTOD) method in September gilt.

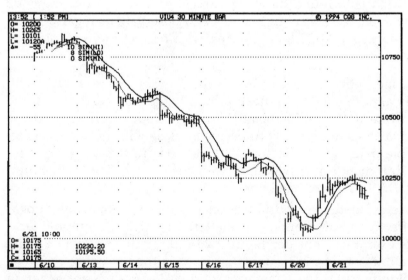

Figure 23-2. The 10/8 moving average channel (MAC) in 30-minute Italian bond.

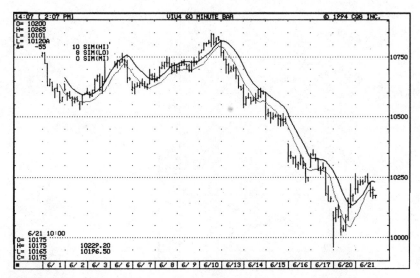

Figure 23-3. The 10/8 MAC in 60-minute Italian bond.

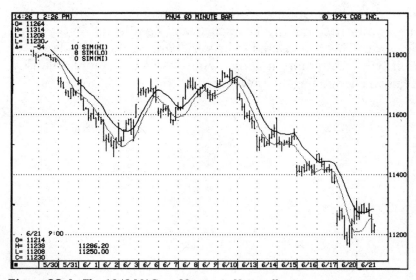

Figure 23-4. The 10/8 MAC on 60-minute Notionell.

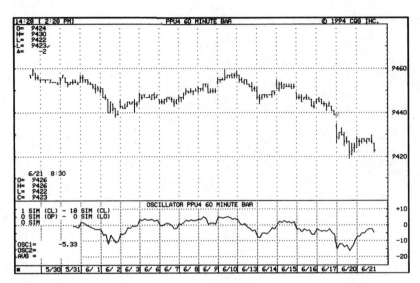

Figure 23-5. A 1/18 oscillator in 60-minute Pibor.

Globex, *do not* use the night session data, since they tend to obscure the gaps. I've found that the gaps are working very well as long as the Globex trading is ignored for the purpose of calculating gap higher or lower openings.

4. Remember that as the trading world grows smaller, we will find ourselves in an international market which will be affected by news all over the world. This is expected to be very beneficial for the day trader, since it will create more market swings as well as more volatility. As you know, change begets opportunity.

24

Twenty Keys to Success as a Day Trader

It is not possible for me to overemphasize the fact that great traders, in particular great day traders, are great because they have mastered the discipline of trading as well as the mechanical techniques. I've placed great emphasis on discipline and feel that since it is undoubtedly the weak link in the chain of trading behavior, no consistent success is possible without it. There are many opinions as to what constitutes discipline. Different traders and different writers will give you distinctly different opinions. My point of view has been tempered and shaped by over 22 years of trading, trading which has exposed me to every conceivable type of market and every conceivable type of news event. This has forced me to develop an arsenal of time-tested procedures which I now share with you. The best way for me to convey this information is by listing the items. So here they are, not necessarily in order of importance:

1. *Find your place.* One of the most important considerations in day trading is for the trader to find his or her place in the vast world of day trading. There are many things a day trader can do, but only so many can be done at one time. I suggest you find one or several techniques which you can relate to well and which you feel particularly confident with. These are the techniques which you should then use in your trading. Use them consistently, day in and day out. You will find that certain techniques work best in certain markets: S&P futures, for example, are especially well-suited to the gap opening systems I have described earlier. T-bond futures are particularly well-suited to the support and resistance, scalping type methods I have discussed. Currency futures, given their sharp and fairly quick moves, are especially well-suited to hit-and-

run trading also discussed earlier. The gap method also works well in currencies but with some variation on the theme. Determine which approaches suit you best and devote your time to those methods consistently and for a reasonable period.

2. *Don't expect immediate results.* Many a trader, in fact, many a day trader, has been sorely disappointed when immediate success was not attainable. I urge you to persevere. Be consistent in giving yourself sufficient time to achieve success. It's one thing to learn how to ride a bicycle by reading a book (which is basically what we're doing here), yet it's a far different thing to actually get on that bicycle and ride it after reading the book.

I assume that most of you have already done quite a bit of trading. Although you may feel that this experience will serve you well, it will as a matter of fact most likely be detrimental, since you come to the market with preconceived notions which may stand in your way. You will need to abandon these ideas in favor of those in this book, provided of course that what I've said makes sense to you. Therefore, it is important to remember that the process will take time. Some failures at first will be necessary. You will need to fall off the bicycle a few times before you can ride it. At first your riding will be shaky and slow. After a while, however, you will feel at home on the day-trading bicycle, and it will take you where you choose to go, provided you follow a smooth road. How long will it take? There is no answer other than perhaps more than 2 weeks and less than 2 years, but these are certainly not hard-and-fast rules. Some individuals can be successful in several weeks, whereas others are still not capable of achieving consistent success as day traders even after many years.

3. *Have minimal expectations.* Some books on positive mental attitude will tell you to have great expectations, but I caution you against it. Do not have great expectations. Expect to lose. Expect that with time you will begin to break even. Expect that with more time you will begin to have profitable results. Do not expect profits, but rather expect that learning the game will cost you tuition both in terms of time and money. There are hundreds if not thousands of traders who came to the markets with great expectations and a fistful of dollars but who left the markets beaten, broke, and broken. If anything, you ought to expect failure while hoping that, through your efforts you can minimize the failures and maximize the successes.

4. *Play your own game.* If you allow yourself to be exposed to and influenced by the many fantastic claims for ultimate trading systems and incredible seminars, then you will be distracted on the road to success. There is nothing wrong with attempting to improve on what you

are doing, but the act of searching, ever searching, tends to distract you from your goal. Don't be side-tracked from your goal. Persevere and ignore the claims as much as you can.

The world of futures trading is constantly barraged by those claiming to have better systems, better methods, fool-proof indicators, outstanding results, and fail-safe methods. Before you give any of these serious attention, make sure that what you're doing is not intrinsically better. Every system you test, every seminar you attend, every piece of software you buy, and every path you take may prove to be a costly excursion away from your final destination. They take time, effort, and money. *And these, my friends, are the most precious commodities in the world.* They are limited resources, not easily replaced. Therefore, I suggest you find a methodology and commit to it for a predetermined length of time. And during this period of time *do not allow yourself to become distracted by anything else, even if it means that you need to close your eyes and ears to the magazines, newspapers, and mail you receive.*

5. *Admit to your losses.* I have stated repeatedly throughout this book that the single worst offense a day trader can commit is to carry a position beyond the end of the trading day. *To do so is to violate the essence of day trading and to risk exposure to everything that a day trader seeks to avoid. Do not, under any circumstances violate this cardinal rule regardless of what the excuse or excuses may be.* If, perchance, you are "locked in" to a position due to a limit move against you, then you have no choice. You could spread a position off (take an opposite position in a different contract month if possible) in order to avoid the exposure; however, there is still danger, even in a spread. You are either a day trader or you are not. If you are not a day trader, that's fine. You must not, however, change horses in midstream since this will, in the long run, not serve you well. In the short run, you may be very pleased with the results. But, in time they will return to haunt you.

In the event of a limit move in your favor, you may be tempted to hold your position overnight, expecting that there will be more profits in the morning. Even this is a dangerous procedure because *a limit move in either direction on any given day does not statistically guarantee follow-through in the same direction on the next day.* My research has shown that over *the next several days* there may be follow through; however, what happens between now and then may wipe you out. I have already given you certain very specific conditions under which a day trade may be kept overnight, but beyond these suggestions, I emphasize once again that a day trade must be closed out by the end of the day.

6. *Set your daily goal as a day trader.* I encourage you to have one simple goal every day of your life as a day trader; *attempt to end the day with*

a profit. Place no dollar amount on the profit or it may distract you. To set a goal too high would be unrealistic and to set a goal too low might be unfair. However, to set another type of goal—the goal of following your rules and being true to your methods—this is the goal of the day trader. If, however, you do need to establish yourself a goal in terms of dollars, then tell yourself that you will strive to end each day with a small profit at the very minimum.

7. *Prepare for the end of the day.* The disciplined day trader knows that the end of the day is, most often, the end of all trades that day. There is a specific time limit on how long a profitable trade may be carried during the day. The end of the day is, after all, the end of the day, and positions *must be closed out.* Some of the techniques I have discussed clearly indicate market exit under very specific circumstances, and others are more adapted to exit on the close of trading. Ideally, a profitable position will be kept for as long as possible. It is not uncommon for market moves to become accentuated toward the end of the session and, therefore, for considerable profit to be derived from your trades as the day draws to an end.

As the end of the day approaches, therefore, I want you to be more and more inclined to take your profit at the slightest indication that the existing trend may reverse itself. Unfortunately, this is, many times, a judgment call rather than an objective formal procedure. An intuitive sense may need to be developed in order to achieve this goal. No matter what some traders may tell you about the tremendous systems they've developed, the fact remains that it is impossible to day trade without some degree of judgment. Some things in the markets just aren't regular—they're random events which have no prescribed method of response. It is my most sincere hope that what you will learn within these pages will help you make such judgment calls successfully.

In view of the above, make certain that as the end of the trading day approaches, you continue to raise your stop loss (mental or actual) closer and closer to the current market price, thereby allowing the market to get you out when the trend reverses. In addition, there are certain types of orders you can use (previously discussed) which can help considerably. *But remember, your goal is to be out by the end of the day.*

8. *Don't let good profits turn into losses.* Many a good day trade has become a bad day trade, by turning from a profit into a loss, due to poor intraday risk management. Please remember the rules I have given you about raising stop losses (mental or otherwise) to the point of breakeven plus commission. This is an important rule which you must not violate. Preservation of capital is quintessential to consistent success as a day trader.

9. *Don't force trades.* Many traders have the personality type that craves action. This fatal flaw causes them to search out trading opportunities where and when none exist. If you have seen no opportunity for day trades but find yourself idly searching through your screens and intraday charts for opportunities, then you are headed for a disaster. If you find yourself looking at markets which you never trade, for opportunities which you have not seen previously in the day, then you are most likely headed for trouble. *Do not attempt to create an opportunity where one does not exist.* Be patient. There will be trades tomorrow or the next day. The market always provides opportunities over time even though none may exist today. *Don't ever, ever force yourself to trade if an opportunity is not readily apparent.*

10. *Don't hesitate.* This is one of the worst enemies of the day trader. The expression "he who hesitates has lost" is more true in the futures markets than anywhere else. Since day trading is encapsulated in a circumscribed period of time, every moment you lose in entering or exiting a position is a moment that may cost you money. If you choose to hesitate then do so with premeditation and calculated caution. *Do not hesitate out of fear or indecision.* Hesitation subsequent to a clear trading signal or opportunity indicates lack of confidence, and lack of confidence indicates that you are not comfortable with your choice of systems and/or methods or with your skills as a day trader. Hesitation can be costly.

11. *Keep a diary.* I have elaborated on this topic earlier but I emphasize it here once again due to the great importance it can play in helping you learn from your mistakes and of course from your successes. A diary should not only be kept, but it should also be referred to both at the end of each trading day and at the beginning of the new day. Refer to everything you did the day before and *learn from it.* Please refer to the examples I have given you previously for specifics.

12. *If you have to watch the markets, then don't trade.* Some of the techniques I have discussed in this book are so totally mechanical that your presence is not required and live price quotes are unnecessary. *Other methods, however, require your presence and close attention.* If a situation arises during the day which requires you to leave your quote system, then either close out your positions immediately or give your broker stop close only or market on close orders. *Do not attempt to keep in touch with the markets by calling frequently for quotes or by using a portable quotation system.* This is not a good way to operate.

13. *When in doubt, stay out.* The old expression "when in doubt, stay out" is particularly appropriate for the day trader. Not all indicators or

signals will be completely clear all the time. Furthermore, some other developments such as news, reports, or short-term fundamentals make signals unclear or market response uncertain. In such cases my best advice is to stay out; do not trade. There will always be plenty of trades, and there is no need to enter a trade unless its potential outcome is relatively clear and free from the erratic influence of news or other fundamental events.

14. *Do your homework.* It never ceases to amaze me how few traders consistently do their market homework. Even though they have developed good market indicators and effective trading techniques, they fail to consistently keep up to date on the markets and allow a good methodology to turn into a bad one, by virtue of their laziness. This makes no sense to me whatsoever. The fact is that if you develop something which works, and if it is making money for you or facilitating your ability to make money, then by all means you ought to continue with it.

Too many traders become complacent about their market studies, fail to do their homework, and then wonder why they lose money. If you intend to succeed, then you must do your homework no matter how simple or complex it may be.

Perhaps you have developed a trading system which requires no homework. This is certainly possible. A number of the techniques described in this book do not require homework. However, you will still need to work on your trading diary, and you will still need to keep in close touch with trading opportunities which may develop during the next trading day. The only way to do this is to study the markets. This is what I mean by homework, and this is why it must be done.

15. *Monitor your performance.* Some traders refuse to monitor their trading results as a form of defense against being distressed by bad results. This is neurotic behavior and should not be engaged in. Always keep close track of your results on a trade-by-trade and day-by-day basis. Know where you stand at all times in order to acquire effective feedback about the techniques you are using. Unless you know where you stand, you will not have sufficient information about how well or how poorly your methods are performing. I suggest you use one of the many computerized accounting programs to keep track of your results, or, at the very minimum, a spreadsheet which is updated manually will certainly do the job. Pay especially close attention to your average winning trade and your average losing trade. Your average winners should be consistently larger than your average losers. If they are not, then you are risking too much and getting too little for your efforts. This is an indication that change is necessary.

Another good reason for keeping track of all your trades and their results is for determining if and when your trading technique, system, or indicators have deteriorated and are in need of change or review. Unless you check your performance you will not be cognizant that change is necessary, other than perhaps a vague feeling that all is not going well.

16. *More complicated is not necessarily synonymous with more profitable.* There is no doubt that you will be tempted many times to use more complicated trading systems. You will be tempted to build more and more rules into your system feeling, erroneously, that your system will work better if it has more rules. You may feel that if your system takes more market variables into consideration, you will trade more profitably. My experience strongly suggests otherwise. With the exception of artificial-intelligence-based systems which can process vast amounts of data in exceedingly complex ways, relating data to market patterns and relationships, adding new inputs or variables to your own analytical techniques does not necessarily improve them and may in fact cause them to deteriorate.

I have found that if there is a relationship between complexity of system and profitability of system, then it may well be an inverse relationship. *The simpler a system is, the more likely it is to be profitable.* So please, don't confuse apparent complexity with profitability.

17. *Beware of market myths.* The markets are forever subject to the emotional influence of traders. Through the years traders have come to believe that certain relationships exist in the markets *when in fact these relationships do not exist at all.* Statistically, few consistent market relationships have persisted over many years. Therefore, be careful not to get caught up in the cycle of hope which perpetuates market myths.

18. *Beware the dangers of pyramiding. Pyramiding* is the act of adding increasingly larger units to your position as a market moves in your favor. Therefore, you may begin by buying one unit and adding two additional units once the trade has moved in your favor. If the trade continues to move in your favor, you may add four new units and then, assuming it continues in your favor you might add six or eight units. The essence of pyramiding is that *increasingly larger positions are added as the trade moves in your favor.* The upside of this methodology is that you will accumulate a very large position consistent with the trend and you will use the capital available in open profits to margin new positions. The danger of pyramiding is that this is a pyramid clearly built upside down. It is heaviest at the top and rests on only one unit at the bottom. It is, therefore, subject to violent collapse at the slightest indication of a trend reversal. If you intend to build a pyramid, then do so by establish-

ing your largest position first and follow it up by successively smaller numbers of units.

19. *Trade active markets only.* Here is a bit of advice I've given you repeatedly throughout the book; however, I cannot stress it too strongly. By trading in active markets only, you will avoid the problems which come with thinly traded markets and the relatively poor price executions which are so common in such markets. As a day trader, you must have liquidity in order to move into and out of your positions easily and without too much slippage. Moreover, if you intend to trade large positions, then liquidity is absolutely essential for success. As a day trader, you do not have the time to wait too long for price executions to be reported to you, nor will you have the time to go back and forth with different price orders in an effort to have your positions either entered or closed out.

Since markets wax and wane in terms of trading activity, you will need to evaluate this on an ongoing basis in order to make certain that you are participating in actively traded markets. If you find yourself trading thin markets and experiencing all the difficulties which go along with such markets, then I assure you that you have no one to blame but yourself since you have violated one of the cardinal rules of day trading.

As this book is being written, the active futures markets are as follows: S&P 500, Treasury bond, Swiss franc, Deustch mark, British pound, crude oil, Eurodollar, and a handful of other futures markets. As you can see, the number of vehicles open to the day trader is rather small. But this, I assure you, is a blessing in disguise. An effective day trader cannot spread him- or herself too thin among too many choices.

20. *Be a contrarian.* Some of the largest intraday moves occur when they are least expected. The general trading public and a vast majority of professionals will be on the wrong side of the market when these moves happen simply because they get blindsided by their collective sentiment. Mob psychology is a very important factor which may be used to the advantage of the day trader. If you find that the market sentiment (see previous discussion of market sentiment) is heavily weighted on one side of the market or another, then watch closely for timing indicators which will give you market entry on the opposite side of majority opinion.

While these are just a few of the important things to remember if you sincerely want to be a successful day trader, they are by no means the only prerequisites to success. I urge you to develop and maintain your own list which is derived from your experiences as a day trader, since your own list will be considerably more meaningful to you. The foregoing is merely a beginning, a base upon which I urge you to build on your own.

Now it's time for you to strike out on your own, and/or to integrate my tools into your trading style. I don't claim to have all the answers, and I don't give you any guarantees other than to tell you that with persistence, patience, and motivation you will succeed. If I can help you, then don't hesitate to contact me at the address previously given. I have learned enough about the markets in my more than 20 years of trading to know that the more I learn, the more there is to learn. And I also know this: *that which has worked best for me is that which is both the most simple to do and the most simple to understand.*

Appendix

Formulae

Stochastic

Fast Stochastic

Fast %K.   The system identifies the highest high, lowest low, and the current *price* (either open, high, low, close, midpoint, or average), for a specified *period* (number of bars.) It subtracts the lowest low from the current *price*, then divides the difference by the range (where the range is the highest high to lowest low). The result becomes the first fast %K value. The system continues to calculate fast %K values by excluding the oldest bar and including the next more recent bar before repeating the above calculation.

Fast %D.   This is a moving average of fast %K values.

Slow Stochastic

Fast %K and Fast %D are calculated as above (not displayed). Slow %K is equal to the fast %D. Slow %D is a moving average of slow %K values.

When *slow stochastic* is selected, the system internally calculates both the fast and slow stochastic; however, only the slow %K and slow %D lines are displayed on the screen.

The following are variables for the two stochastic studies above:

S Stoch   *Period* and *price* used for the calculation of an unseen Fast %K

S Stoch %K	*Period* and *type* of average used for the calculation of an unseen Fast %D. This value is also slow %K
S Stoch %D	*Period* and *type* of average used for the calculation of slow %D
F Stoch	*Period* and *price* used for the calculation of a fast %K
F Stoch %D	*Period* and *type* of average used for the calculation of a fast %D.

Note that the *price* for the calculation of %K is usually the *close*. The *period* and *type* of moving average for the calculation of the %D is usually *3-period smoothed*. Other *prices*, *periods*, and *types* may be entered in the study variables setup.

Smoothed Moving Average

The following indicator formulae are reprinted with permission of CQG Inc. These are the indicator calculations used on my CQG System One. These formulae can be programmed into your computer, computed by hand, or programmed into Omega TradeStation of SystemWriter.

A *smoothed moving average* differs from a *simple moving average* in terms of the value that is subtracted before each calculation. In a simple moving average, the oldest value is subtracted. In a smoothed moving average the previous smoothed average value is subtracted. The first value for a smoothed moving average is determined by the formula SM1. It is plotted on the chart at the third bar from the left side of the screen.

$$SM1 = \frac{\text{Price 1 + price 2 + price 3}}{\text{Period}}$$

The next value would be determined by formula SM2. It is plotted at the fourth bar from the left side of the screen.

$$SM2 = \frac{\text{Previous sum} - \text{previous avg} + \text{price 4}}{\text{Period}}$$

For the calculation of SM2, *previous sum* is the sum of price 1 + price 2 + price 3; *previous avg* is the value of SM1.

The next value would be determined by formula SM3. It is plotted at the fifth bar from the left side of the screen.

$$SM3 = \frac{\text{Previous sum} - \text{previous avg} + \text{price 5}}{\text{Period}}$$

Subsequent values would be determined by subtracting the previous avg from the previous sum, adding the next more recent price, then dividing by the period.

Index

About the Author

Jake Bernstein is an internationally recognized trader, author, and researcher. He has written over 27 books and studies on futures trading and has spoken at investment and trading seminars the world over. He has been a guest on numerous business radio and television programs including Wall Street Week.